Fiscal neutrality

toward

economic growth

Analysis of a taxation principle

Economics handbook series
Seymour E. Harris, editor

The board of advisors
Neil W. Chamberlain, Yale University—Labor
John M. Culbertson, University of Wisconsin—Monetary Theory
Seymour E. Harris, Harvard University—International Economics, Social Security; all other areas
Franco Modigliani, Massachusetts Institute of Technology—Economic Theory
Richard A. Musgrave, Harvard University—Public Policy
Marc Nerlove, Yale University—Econometrics and Mathematical Economics

Fiscal neutrality

toward

economic growth

Analysis of a taxation principle

Edmund S. Phelps
Associate Professor of Economics,   Yale University

McGraw-Hill Book Company
New York, St. Louis, San Francisco, Toronto, London, Sydney

Fiscal neutrality toward economic growth
Analysis of a taxation principle

Library of Congress Catalog Card Number 65-21575

49780

1234567890 MP 7210698765

to my parents

Preface

Two schools of thought exist concerning public policy toward economic growth. There are a few economists who appear to believe that, in a capitalist economy, the consumer, through competitive markets, decides the rate of private investment and hence the rate of growth, that the government plays no role in determining private investment. But in the mixed capitalist systems of the present day, this view must assume, contrary to modern and classical economic theory, that fiscal and monetary policies are ineffective in controlling the mix between private investment and consumption.

The other school of thought holds that the consumer cannot be assumed to choose the preferred investment rate since the government may bias the market solution in some way by its fiscal and monetary policies. These economists go on to argue that because the government controls the growth rate, the government—or the people by some political means—ought to decide the rate of growth. But whether or not it is correct, this conclusion is a *non sequitur*.

The question arises as to whether there is not a tenable middle ground. Is there some fiscal principle—specifically, some rule of taxation—the pursuit of which, in conjunction with the operation of perfect markets, would cause consumers to choose the preferred rate of investment? This book examines one such principle, namely, what we call *fiscal neutrality* toward economic growth. The aim and structure of the book is set forth in detail in Chapter 1.

The book was begun in 1962–1963 when I was visiting associate professor of economics at the Massachusetts Institute of Technology. There I had the benefit of many stimulating discussions, especially those with Francis M. Bator, E. Cary Brown, Franco Modigliani, Paul A. Samuelson, and Robert M. Solow. The book was completed in 1963–1964 at Yale University, where my research was jointly financed by the Cowles Foundation for Research in Economics and the Economic Growth Center. At Yale I had the opportunity to discuss various subjects relating to this book with William C. Brainard, Arthur M. Okun, and James Tobin.

I should like to thank also Kenneth J. Arrow, Arnold C. Harberger, and Richard R. Nelson for reading and commenting upon the first draft and for encouraging me to publish. Finally, Marcus Miller, a Yale University graduate student in economics, helped to improve the style.

Since there may be much that is controversial in this book, I should like to emphasize that none of these persons necessarily agrees with any part of this book; therefore none of them should be implicated in the final product.

Edmund S. Phelps

Contents

Chapter 1

The nature

and significance

of government controls

over growth

It is frequently asserted that in contemporary capitalistic economies the consumer necessarily is sovereign over the rate of investment, that it is he alone—not his government—who can and does decide the rate of investment and hence the rate of growth. Believers in this proposition fall into two groups: those political conservatives who are pleased to believe that consumers rather than the government choose the investment rate; and those socialists who say that capitalism is inferior to socialism because under capitalism the government cannot determine the investment rate.

This belief in the inability of the government to influence investment in a capitalistic economy flies in the face of modern as well as classical economic theory. The truth (as far as we know it) is that in contemporary capitalistic economies subject to ordinary fiscal and monetary controls, the government has considerable influence over the investment rate. These controls, moreover, are used all the time, wittingly or unwittingly, for good or ill. In the first part of this chapter we shall review their nature and scope.

1.1 The Nature and Scope of Government Control over Investment

It is clear that, by its expenditure decision, the government exercises direct control over the volume of public investment. This part of the present chapter will be concerned with the more subtle matter of how the government exercises indirect control over the volume of private investment undertaken.[1]

1.1.1 Classical thought

Recognition of the power of the state to alter the rate of private investment is as old as classical economics. The classical economists believed that a budgetary deficit would reduce private investment and thus slow the growth of the economy and, by implication, that a budgetary surplus would increase the growth of the economy.

The fundamental classical objection to deficit finance—that it sets back the growth of capital—was stated clearly by Ricardo. After denying that taxation to service an already existing debt is a real burden (on the ground that it is a transfer from one citizen to another) he wrote:[2] "From what I have said it must not be inferred that I consider the system of borrowing as the best calculated to defray the extraordinary expenses of the state. It is a system which tends to make us less

---

[1] If the government follows the rule of making public investment up to the point where its social rate of return is equal to the social rate of return on private investment—a rule that on certain assumptions must be followed if dynamical efficiency is to be achieved—then the volume of public investment undertaken will be determined implicitly by the volume of private investment which the government causes to be undertaken.

[2] David Ricardo, *Principles of Political Economy and Taxation* (New York: E. P. Dutton, Everyman's Library, 1911), p. 162. The remainder of the passage is interesting, though difficult to understand:

"If the expenses of a war be 40 millions per annum and the share which a man would have to contribute towards that annual expense were £100, he would endeavor, on being called upon for his portion, to save speedily the £100 from his income. By the system of loans he is called upon to pay only the interest of this £100, or £5 per annum, and considers that he does enough by saving this £5 from

thrifty—to blind us to our real situation." The suggestion here is that
had the "extraordinary" expenditure been financed by an increase of
taxes, consumers would have felt poorer by the amount of the additional taxes and would have reduced their consumption accordingly;
the reduction of consumption would have released resources for government use and thus reduced or eliminated any diversion of resources
away from the investment sector.

The basis for Ricardo's objection to deficit finance as shown by this
quotation is interesting. Deficit finance acts to "blind us to our real
situation." This statement may be the first expression of the doctrine
which we shall later describe as *neutralism*, a doctrine which states
that government taxes and debt ought to be at levels which convey to
consumers the opportunity costs of the resources diverted from private
to public use.

The classical proposition that, given the level of government expenditures, a reduction of taxes would stimulate consumption and
thereby reduce investment and growth was based upon Say's law,
according to which aggregate output always tends to the full-employment level whatever the government's fiscal policy and whatever the
supply of money. The interest rate was postulated to rise or fall so as
to equate investment demand to the supply of total saving at the full-
employment level of income. A tax reduction which stimulated consumption demand, hence aggregate demand and the transaction
demand for money, would generate an excess demand for money.
Because the demand for money was supposed to be perfectly inelastic
with respect to the interest rate, the interest rate would tend to rise
without limit as long as aggregate demand, and hence the demand for
money, was above its equilibrium level. But the rise of the interest rate
would reduce investment demand until finally investment demand had
fallen so much that aggregate demand had returned to its equilibrium
level. Thus the new equilibrium would be one in which the interest rate

his expenditure, and then deludes himself with the belief that he is as rich as before.
The whole nation, by reasoning and acting in this manner, save only the interest
of 40 millions or two millions; and thus not only lose all the interest or profit which
40 millions of capital, employed productively, would afford, but also 38 millions,
the difference between their savings and expenditure [pp. 162–163]."

was higher than before, investment being smaller and consumption larger—with aggregate output again at its full-employment level.[1]

1.1.2 Crude Keynesianism

Keynes's *General Theory* revolutionized the economist's view of budgetary deficits.[2] Keynes denied that the interest rate would automatically adjust to keep the economy at full employment in the face of changes in aggregate demand. The Keynesian analysis proceeds as follows: Suppose the economy were initially at full employment, with the government running a budgetary deficit. If the government raised taxes in an effort to achieve a budgetary balance, consumption demand would contract; however, the interest rate, while it would fall, would not fall sufficiently to return aggregate output to the full-employment level. This follows from Keynes's rejection of the classical postulate of a perfectly interest-inelastic demand for money. He reasoned that a fall of the interest rate would encourage more persons to bet on a subsequent rise of interest rates, hence a capital loss on nonmoney assets, and thus would encourage more persons to hold money as a "speculation." Thus a fall of the interest rate would increase the quantity of money demanded at any given level of aggregate income. An increase of taxes, by reducing aggregate demand and income and creating an excess supply of money, would cause the interest rate to fall. But because of the supposed interest elasticity of the demand for money, the interest rate would *not* come to rest only when investment demand had risen sufficiently to restore full employment; it would come to rest as soon as the increase in quantity of money demanded which was induced by the fall of interest rates just offset the reduction in the quantity of money demanded for transactions purposes which was induced by the fall of aggregate income. Thus the new equilibrium produced by the tax increase would be one of lower income, employment, and consumption; and investment demand, despite the fall of interest

---

[1] The price level remains constant during this equilibration process. Yet price flexibility is implied by the classical system, for the real value of any given money supply is assumed to be equated to the full-employment transaction demand for real money balances.

[2] J. M. Keynes, *The General Theory of Employment, Interest and Money* (London: Macmillan & Co., Ltd., 1936).

rates, would also be lower if the reduction of sales discouraged investment.[1]

This analysis pointed to the conclusion that in the absence of any monetary action, a tax increase was a doubtful means of stimulating investment; moreover it was a means too costly in terms of unemployment and the immediate loss of income. The possibility that monetary policy could be employed to stimulate investment demand sufficiently to offset the tax-induced reduction of consumption demand was, indeed, considered by Keynes. Many expositors of Keynes assumed, however, perhaps for simplicity, that monetary policy was entirely ineffective. The result was the so-called principle of functional finance (a term first used by Abba Lerner), which has been nicely summarized by Franco Modigliani:[2]

Given the full-employment output, say $\bar{X}$, and given the share of this output which it is appropriate to allocate for government use, say G^*, there is a maximum amount of output that is left available for the private sector, say $\bar{P} = \bar{X} - G^*$. Now the private sector demand for output, say P, is a function of income and taxes, say $P = \varphi(X,T)$, with $\partial P/\partial T < 0$. Taxes are then to be set at that level, say $\bar{T}$, which satisfies the equation $\varphi(\bar{X},T) = \bar{P}$. A higher level of taxes would generate unemployment and a lower level would generate inflation, both evils which it is the task of government to avoid. $\bar{T}$ may turn out to be larger than G^*, or even perchance just equal to G^*.

According to this doctrine, then, the use of government's fiscal tool, tax collection, must serve the social objective of full employment. In this view, the government is not really in simultaneous control of employment and investment, for the volume of taxes collected affects investment only as it affects the level of income and employment. To be sure, we should note that the government may still manipulate the tax *structure* in such a way as to stimulate or retard investment. But the effect of the tax structure on the distribution of income must also be considered. If the government hitches the tax structure to the wagon

[1] If prices and wage rates are flexible, then it is conceivable that, as argued by Pigou, the economy will return to full employment in the long run. But that long run might be a long time in coming.

[2] Franco Modigliani, "Long-run Implications of Alternative Fiscal Policies and the Burden of the National Debt," *Economic Journal*, vol. 71 (December, 1961), pp. 730–755. (The quotation, p. 733, contains a number of typographical errors which have been corrected in the text.)

of optimal income distribution, it will find itself in the position of having too few policy tools (or, to preserve the metaphor, too few horses) to control both the investment rate and the level of employment.

1.1.3 Sophisticated Keynesianism

As mentioned earlier, the principle according to which there is only one tax level which will produce the desired level of employment rests on the postulate that monetary action cannot be substituted for fiscal action as a means of controlling aggregate demand. According to Keynes, however, there is a range within which the central bank could raise or lower the rate of interest at which people are willing to lend. If interest rates are inside this range, an increase of taxes, which reduces aggregate demand, can be offset by a reduction of the interest rate, which increases aggregate demand. Thus the government is confronted with a choice between fiscal and monetary means of controlling the level of employment.

The choice is significant because each option has different implications for the rate of growth. Since, at a given level of income, a tax increase bears down primarily on consumption, an increase of tax rates coupled with a reduction of interest rates which just maintains income at the desired level will reduce consumption and raise investment. Thus a combination of "easy money" and "tight fiscal policy" is conducive to high investment and rapid growth; "tight money" offset by "fiscal ease" produces high consumption and slow growth.[1,2]

---

[1] If monetary policy works only after a lag, so that investment demand is not immediately susceptible to policy, then there is initially only one tax level compatible with full employment. But there remains a choice of fiscal paths over time, a choice between easy money in the present with tight fiscal policy in the future and tight money in the present with easy fiscal policy in the future.

[2] Ordinarily the argument is that the two tools of money supply and taxes are sufficient to achieve the two objectives of full employment and the desired consumption-investment mix. This analysis refers to a model in which prices and wage rates are rigid. In a flexible wage-price model, output will settle down to its full-employment equilibrium level whatever the government's use of its two policy tools. In such a model, however, the government may still employ its two tools to serve two objectives, namely, the price level and the consumption-investment mix. Thus the government could use its fiscal and monetary tools to achieve a price level less than last year's price level (a deflationary price policy), together with a specified rate of growth by means of relatively tight money *and* tight taxa-

These considerations led Paul Samuelson[1] to make an optimistic pronouncement in 1955: "With proper fiscal and monetary policies, our economy can have full employment and whatever rate of capital formation and growth it wants." Plainly, Samuelson was exaggerating when he said "whatever." Yet his optimism about the government's power over the rate of investment contrasted sharply with the opinion prevailing in the thirties and forties. For while Keynes himself held that normally the central bank could lower the rate of interest and that any reduction of the rate of interest would stimulate investment demand, he believed that investment demand could not be much stimulated by this means.

First, Keynes suspected that investment demand was not very interest elastic. If taxes were increased sufficiently to cause a large fall of consumption demand (at the desired level of income), a negative (and hence infeasible) rate of interest might be required to stimulate an increase of investment demand equal to the fall of consumption demand.

Second, he believed that with a relatively low, but positive, level of interest, the speculative demand for money could become completely elastic. Hence, the monetary authorities might not be able to reduce the interest rate to the required level even if that required level were positive. In attempting to lower the interest rate to the required level, the speculative demand for money might increase to such an extent that the central bank could purchase all the government bonds outstanding and reduce reserve requirements of banks until they were no longer binding and still not succeed in driving the interest rate down enough. To accomplish its task, the central bank would have to make direct loans to private firms or purchase private securities; but this last resort was not considered practical.

---

tion, or to achieve a price level greater than last year's (an inflationary price trend), together with the same specified growth rate by means of relatively easy money *and* easy taxation.

[1] Paul A. Samuelson, "The New Look in Tax and Fiscal Policy," *Federal Tax Policy for Economic Growth and Stability*, Subcommittee on Tax Policy, Joint Committee on the Economic Report, 84th Cong., 1955, pp. 229–234.

1.1.4 The range of possible investment rates consistent with full employment

The shift from the Keynesian pessimism of the thirties to the optimism expressed by Samuelson in the fifties can be explained by postwar developments both historical and theoretical in nature. The comparative buoyancy of investment demand in the postwar period was perhaps the most important cause of the new optimism. This buoyancy occurred despite the fact that interest rates were typically higher in the postwar period than in the thirties and forties. Certain theoretical developments also increased the optimism of economists concerning the effectiveness with which the monetary authorities could alter the rate of investment.

First, Keynes's supposition of inelastic interest-rate expectations, which was the basis for the interest elasticity of the demand for money in the *General Theory*, was questioned. Keynes supposed that any fall of interest rates would be regarded by the public as temporary and would be followed by a rise of interest rates and hence a fall of securities prices; this expectation would cause people to sell securities in response to a fall of interest rates, and such sales would drive their prices down and interest rates up. Therefore, massive monetary operations were thought to be necessary to achieve a modest change of interest rates. But should people become convinced that the reduction of interest rates was permanent (as they presumably would if the monetary authorities engaged in a sustained drive to reduce interest rates), they would then bid more vigorously for securities and thus force interest rates to lower levels. The demand for money, therefore, may be considerably less interest elastic in the long run than in the short run.

Indeed, the only reasons for supposing that there is any interest elasticity at all in the long run is that, at a higher interest rate, there would be a greater desire to economize on money—people would be induced to hold securities over a part of their income period despite the cost and nuisance of having to sell them when money was needed for transactions—and, at a higher rate of interest, there would be more compensation for holding risky interest-bearing assets in preference to money. Neither consideration suggests that the demand for money is extremely interest elastic. Hence it seems likely that a given reduction of interest rates could be accomplished by a smaller increase of the money supply than was supposed by Keynes and his followers.

Suppose we grant that the central bank can depress to a very low level the rate of return at which the community is willing to invest. There remains the question: How much additional investment would take place before the rate of return fell to the new and lower level? This is essentially the question of the interest elasticity of investment demand.

Keynes, as we have mentioned above, believed that the rate of return on investment would decrease sharply with additional investment; it was on this ground that he considered investment demand quite inelastic with respect to the interest rate. The belief was based on the feeling that there was little substitutability between capital and labor. In fact great interest was shown after World War II in the models of Roy Harrod and Evsey Domar, which postulate no variability whatsoever in the proportions in which capital goods and labor can be combined. According to these models, if there were just sufficient capital to employ the initial labor force, then investment in excess of the level necessary to employ new workers coming into the labor force would contribute nothing to the growth rate and could not be induced in any case since its rate of return would be zero, while investment short of the necessary level would bring about unemployment. There was, therefore, just one full-employment investment rate and growth rate.

But by the mid-fifties this pessimistic view of the possibility of encouraging substantial capital deepening by reducing interest rates met with dissent. James Tobin, Robert Solow, and Trevor Swan[1] presented growth models in which capital and labor could be employed in variable proportions. In the case of the Cobb-Douglas function, for example—it was to this production function that Solow and Swan paid special attention—there is no limit to the capital investment that could contribute to increased capacity: every 1 per cent increase of the tangi-

[1] James Tobin, "A Dynamic Aggregative Model," *Journal of Political Economy*, vol. 62 (April, 1955), pp. 103–115.

Robert M. Solow, "A Contribution to the Theory of Economic Growth," *Quarterly Journal of Economics*, vol. 70 (February, 1956), pp. 65–94.

Trevor W. Swan, "Economic Growth and Capital Accumulation," *Economic Record*, vol. 32 (November, 1956), pp. 334–361.

ble capital stock will reduce the marginal productivity of capital by only β per cent, where β is the elasticity of output with respect to labor.

While several investigators have obtained good statistical fits of the Cobb-Douglas function to United States data,[1] there is still much uncertainty about the degree of substitutability between capital and labor. Recent theoretical research has suggested, however, that increased investment may contribute to productivity in ways other than *capital deepening* (the increase of capital per man). We refer to *vintage models* in which the productivity of new capital goods exceeds the productivity of old capital goods by virtue of *investment-embodied* technical progress. In particular, we have in mind that sort of vintage model in which, while there may exist a choice of machines of differing labor intensities which can be constructed, once a machine has been constructed, there is no possibility of varying the number of workers manning the machine short of withdrawing labor from it altogether and thus idling the machine.

In one particular vintage model of this sort, a model in which it is supposed that the labor intensity of new machinery is variable and can be described by a Cobb-Douglas function, the author has demonstrated that an increase of investment will contribute to capacity output, not only by making more capital available, but also, in the long run, by that raising of productivity which results from the lengthening of the profitable operating life of machinery. The latter phenomenon the author called *capital lengthening*.[2]

In another vintage model in which there is no substitutability between capital and labor either with respect to machines under current construction or with respect to already existing machines, it has been shown that while additional investment must lead to the displacement of an amount of old capital sufficient to release the amount of labor required to man the new investments, this reallocation of labor from old machines to new machines raises aggregate output (by virtue of the greater efficiency of new machines). We refer to as yet unpub-

---

[1] See, for example, Robert M. Solow, "Technical Progress, Capital Formation and Economic Growth," *American Economic Review: Annual Proceedings of the American Economic Association*, vol. 52 (May, 1962), pp. 76–86.

[2] Edmund S. Phelps, "Substitution, Fixed Proportions, Growth and Distribution," *International Economic Review*, vol. 4, no. 3 (September, 1963), pp. 265–288.

lished work by Robert Solow, James Tobin, Christian von Weiszäcker, and Menahem Yaari. This phenomenon, which can be described as a reduction of the mean age of capital goods in use, Solow has called *capital quickening*.

Hence, while the class of vintage models has not been fully explored, such investigation as there has been suggests that investment could in practice be increased (decreased) without a drastic fall (rise) of the rate of return, even if there is little substitutability between capital and labor. This suggests in turn that variations of the interest rate would have significant effects upon the volume of investment undertaken.

It is probably true to say, therefore, that economists are currently somewhat more optimistic about the range of investment levels consistent with full employment from which the fiscal and monetary authorities can choose. But there is, finally, another issue which deserves some discussion. It is sometimes alleged that the rate of investment, at least investment in tangible capital if not investment in new technology and investment in human capital, has little effect upon the growth rate. If this were so, should the investment rate be of serious concern to the government?

It is true that if the gross marginal productivity of investment were zero, i.e., variation of the investment rate had no effect upon the economy's capacity to produce in the future, then fiscal and monetary policies need not be concerned with the rate of investment; the rate of investment by private producers would necessarily be zero whatever the fiscal-monetary environment. But such a world has never existed: in it the rate of return to investment and hence the real rate of interest would be minus 100 per cent.[1]

It is more plausible to suppose, for the sake of argument, that the net rate of return to investment is zero, that the sacrifice of one unit of consumption in the present would increase future capacity only enough to permit an increase of one unit of future consumption. In this case it is not likely that there would be private investment, but there could be if the fiscal and monetary authorities created an inflationary environment making negative the rate of return on the holding of money. And

---

[1] The (one-period) social rate of return to investment is defined as $(-\Delta C_1/\Delta C_0)$ $- 1$, where C_0 is present consumption and C_1 is consumption next period; C_2, C_3, . . . are to be held constant.

in this case the rate of investment produced by fiscal and monetary policies would be of concern. For while "lifetime" consumption could not be increased by a sacrifice of present consumption, the timing of lifetime consumption would be affected. Therefore, the rate of investment has welfare consequences even if its rate of return is zero (or negative). As long as different fiscal-monetary policies produce different rates of investment, the choice of a fiscal-monetary policy mix must be a matter of concern, however slight the effect of the decision on the rate of growth.[1]

In fact, of course, the social rate of return to investment net of depreciation and obsolescence is far greater than zero. Recent estimates of the net rate of return to tangible investment in the United States are in the neighborhood of 14 per cent.[2,3] Similar estimates for West Germany have been obtained by Solow. And there is cause for believing that the social rates of return to investment in human capital (expenditures on education and technical training) and investment in new technology (expenditures on research) are even higher. Presumably, private rates of return to these investments are about as large as, perhaps much larger than, the private rate of return to tangible investment.[4] If so, then, in view of the important externalities generated by the former kinds of investment, their social rates of return may be very high indeed.

1.2 The Significance of Government Controls over Investment

Many economists, denying the proposition that the consumer—through the market mechanism—decides the growth rate in a capitalistic econ-

[1] The rate of investment could be a matter of indifference only in the bizarre case in which the transformation curve relating maximum future consumption to the level of present consumption is coincidental with the social indifference curve relating present to future consumption (e.g., the two curves are coincidental negatively sloped straight lines). But even this is not sufficient for, in an infinite-horizon model, investment could be permanently too high and thus produce a consumption path dominated by the consumption path produced by a path of uniformly smaller investments.

[2] Edmund S. Phelps, "The New View of Investment: A Neoclassical Analysis," *Quarterly Journal of Economics*, vol. 76 (November, 1962), p. 566.

[3] Robert M. Solow, *Capital Theory and the Rate of Return* (Amsterdam: North Holland Publishing Company, 1963).

[4] See Gary S. Becker, "Underinvestment in College Education," *American Economic Review: Annual Proceedings of the American Economic Association*, vol. 50 (May, 1960), pp. 346–354.

omy subject to fiscal and monetary controls, go on to make a very different assertion. They contend that the market solution can never be relied upon to express consumers' true preferences for growth, because the market solution is contaminated by the way in which the government elects to use its fiscal and monetary controls. The assertion is that the market solution in principle cannot provide any reliable indication of consumer preferences, since the government may have biased that solution in one way or another.

Those who make this assertion conclude that the aggregate investment decision must be "political."[1] In their view, the government has the following choice: Either it must set tax levels arbitrarily, perhaps according to some shibboleth such as "balance the budget," or it must set tax levels consciously so as to achieve the desired rate of investment and rate of growth. A government interested in economic welfare will adopt an *investment policy* or *growth policy*.

There are, perhaps, two ways in which these investment targets might be determined in a democratic society. Some economists apparently wish the government to gather, by survey or experiment, information on the intertemporal preferences of the individuals in the society. This centralized utility information would be used to construct a social welfare function. The government would then employ its fiscal and monetary controls to engineer the investment rate implied by the maximization of social welfare. But probably everyone has misgivings about the practicality of such an approach.

The other approach would use the democratic electoral process. Thus Samuelson writes: "This [governmental] power over the community's rate of capital formation should constitute a sobering responsibility for the voters in any modern democracy."[2] The statement appears to assert that if an optimal rate of investment is to be achieved, it must be by means of a voting process through which the public expresses its preferences among investment rates or growth rates. It suggests that there is no way other than political expression by which the public can make the growth rate accord with its preferences; that, in particular, it is not possible for the public to express its preferences for growth through the market mechanism.

[1] Abba P. Lerner, *The Economics of Control* (New York: The Macmillan Company, 1945), p. 262.

[2] Paul A. Samuelson, *Economics: An Introductory Analysis*, 5th ed. (New York: McGraw-Hill Book Company, 1961), p. 654.

While we are critical of the position just described—the purpose of this book is to examine a different principle for determining the level of taxes—we wish to dissociate ourselves from two reactions which this position frequently induces. The prospect of a national growth policy designed by the central government is often viewed as a dagger at the throat of capitalism. The truth, however, is that all the outward and visible signs of capitalism—at least the kind of controlled capitalism of the present day—would be unaffected by a shift from an arbitrary tax policy to a tax (and monetary) program intended to achieve a certain targeted rate of aggregate investment. Note especially that *free choice*, the ability of the individual consumer to decide what portion of his disposable income to consume, would not be impaired.

Another reaction is based on the contention that a national growth policy is necessarily incompatible with "consumer sovereignty." Individual preferences between consuming in the present and consuming in the future will have no sway, it is argued. But there is no reason why the government could not adopt that growth policy which it believes best caters to the tastes of the population. There seem to be no a priori incompatibility between growth policy and consumer sovereignty. Surely, a growth policy which is intended to produce the growth path which the government believes the public wants is likely to come closer to satisfying community preferences than an arbitrary tax policy which bears no relation to those preferences.

The issue we do take with the position described above is not over the possible desirability of a growth policy but with the proposition that a government interested in economic welfare *must* have a growth policy in the sense of precise or loose investment targets (or growth-rate targets). We agree that the market mechanism does not necessarily indicate consumer preferences for growth; it should be clear from the discussion earlier in this chapter that the government may use its controls over investment to bias the market solution. But we contend that under certain circumstances, there are fiscal principles which, if applied by the government, would allow the community to realize its preferences for growth through the market mechanism. In these special circumstances, we shall argue, there is no need for expression of preferences through a political process; there is no need for a growth policy.

To state our contention somewhat more carefully: On certain conditions regarding preferences, technology, the perfectness of markets, and the way the population changes, adherence to a certain principle of taxation will cause the market mechanism to produce a growth path of private consumption goods which is Pareto-optimal from the standpoint of the present generation.[1] This fiscal principle, which governs the amount and kind of taxes to be levied, involves such variables as the present value of present and planned government expenditures and the size of the government debt. It does not involve the rate of investment, nor does it require centralized utility information or indications of public growth preferences as expressed at the polls.

That there is, at least under some circumstances, such a Pareto-optimal principle of taxation should not be surprising. Consider the somewhat analogous problem of the atemporal (or "static") allocation of resources among various private consumption goods. Economists recognize that when there are public goods, decreasing-cost phenomena, and externalities, the government needs to intervene with government expenditures if a Pareto optimum is to be achieved. But if there is a residue of private consumption goods for which there are perfect markets and which give off no externalities, then we recognize that the government does not, in order to achieve a Pareto-optimal mix of private consumption goods, need a "consumption policy" guided by centralized utility information, nor does it need to submit alternative consumption mixes to a vote. Despite the fact that the government, through its power to tax the production and consumption of various private consumption goods at different rates, can *control* the consumption mix, the government need not *decide* the consumption mix. The principle of taxation to be followed in the traditional one-period model of atemporal allocation among private consumption goods is well known: the government should levy only lump-sum taxes (in sufficient quantity to finance its expenditures). In the absence of externalities and market imperfections (affecting these private consumption goods), such a tax policy will leave prices equal to marginal social costs and thus

---

[1] By such a path we mean one having the property that with the program of government-supplied goods held fixed, no reallocation of resources could make anyone of the present generation better off over his lifetime without making one or more persons of the present generation worse off over their lifetime. By the present generation we mean the population of income earners living at the present time.

permit a Pareto-optimal resource allocation among private consumption goods.[1]

If it is not valid to argue that because the government (by virtue of its choice among kinds of taxes) has power over the mix of private consumption goods, the government "therefore" needs a consumption policy, the question arises: Is it valid to argue that because the government (by virtue of its choice among the kinds and levels of taxes) has power over the rate of investment, the government "therefore" needs a growth policy? We think not. We believe it should be asked whether or not the growth problem can be solved by the application of fiscal principles instead of by the adoption of a growth policy.

The fiscal principle to be investigated here we call the *principle of fiscal neutrality*. We shall say that tax policy is *neutral* if it produces the same allocation of resources (among consumption goods, among people, and between aggregate consumption and investment) as would be produced if there were no government treasury, hence no taxes and government debt, but only a government agency to conscript resources for use in the production of public goods and an agency to redistribute wealth so as to achieve the desired distribution of lifetime income. (We refer, of course, to efficient conscription: The government would conscript that set of resources, among all sets which will suffice to produce the programmed public goods, which entails the least reduction of private output, i.e., which has the smallest opportunity cost.)

This principle is of considerable interest. In the last chapter we shall show that if market imperfections (rather broadly interpreted) and externalities are absent and if generations follow one another in a special way, then a neutral tax policy would yield a growth path of private consumption goods which is Pareto-optimal from the standpoint of the present generation.

Two questions may occur to the reader at this point. First, he will recognize that a conscription system is like a system of lump-sum taxes in that it does not "distort" the allocation of resources among consump-

[1] We are not concerned in this passage nor elsewhere in this book with the question of the Pareto-optimal allocation of government-supplied goods. We take the amounts supplied of these goods as fixed. Where we use the term "fiscal" in this book, we refer to the functions of the "fisc," i.e., the treasury (its taxing and borrowing), not the activities of the expenditure-making branch of government.

tion goods and between consumption and saving. Hence a neutral fiscal policy, which imitates an efficient conscription system, may require the use of lump-sum taxes (and perhaps bar the use of any other kind of tax). But lump-sum taxation, he knows, is not "feasible." What interest, therefore, can there be in a neutral tax policy? Our answer is that, while the lack of lump-sum taxes makes neutrality not generally possible, it is still possible to approximate to a neutral policy by means of other kinds of taxes. This is discussed in some detail in the next chapter.

Second, the reader will recognize that externalities and a variety of market imperfections prevail in real market economies so that a neutral policy is unlikely to be Pareto-optimal. Why then study fiscal neutrality? In part the answer is that these market imperfections and externalities may not be very important. No doubt economists will differ in their appraisals of the importance of these imperfections. If they are not very important, then in some circumstances a neutral policy may be a fair approximation to an optimal policy. And if we know how these imperfections distort investment and saving decisions, we can infer in what manner a neutral policy should be modified.

It may be remarked in passing that economists quite frequently cite this or that imperfection as evidence that capitalistic economies grow too slowly, that they save and invest too little. These writers appear to have carried over a model of capitalism without fiscal and monetary controls to actual economies in which the government, through such controls, exerts an influence on the rate of investment. The fact is that the externalities and market imperfections usually cited tell us little or nothing about the defects of actual tax policy and the resulting investment rate; they tell us about the defects of a neutral tax policy. How do the critics of the growth rate know that fiscal policies have not compensated or even overcompensated (unwittingly to be sure) for the imperfections cited?[1]

---

[1] It can be correctly argued, for example, that if certain kinds of investment generate external returns while other kinds do not, then tax policies which treat these different kinds of investments alike cannot be Pareto-optimal. But this proposition is different from the proposition that because there are external returns to certain kinds of investment, the resulting growth rate will be too small; whether the resulting growth rate is too small (because investment *in toto* is too small) will depend upon the government's tax policy. It can be argued only that

Our belief, therefore, is that the concept of fiscal neutrality toward growth is an interesting one and deserves exploration, even though exact fiscal neutrality is not feasible and even though market imperfections and externalities make exact neutrality nonoptimal. In the end, we are unable to recommend adoption of a neutral fiscal policy. Nevertheless, investigations of fiscal principles (neutrality being just one) which offer an alternative to the adoption of a growth policy should be welcomed.

We can provide now a brief outline of the topics in the chapters which follow. In the next chapter we examine the nature of neutral fiscal policy in a simple barter economy. It is shown there that neutrality exists when taxes are lump-sum and the tax level is such as to make the present discounted value of current and future net taxes expected by the community equal to the sum of the initial government debt and the present discounted value of the program of planned government expenditures (net of governmental user charges). Some of the questions considered in the chapter are: Does a government debt preclude neutrality, or can an initial public debt be "neutralized" by appropriate taxation? Can the debt be neutralized by non-lump-sum taxes? Does neutrality require that the debt be retired—immediately or gradually? More generally, does neutral taxation demand a budgetary surplus or deficit? And how does the neutral financing of government investments which pay for themselves (through user charges) differ from the neutral financing of government investments in "public" capital goods for which no user charges should be made?

Chapter 3 investigates fiscal neutrality in a money economy subject to the monetary controls of a government-owned central bank. It is shown that only government debt held outside the central bank should be neutralized and that this debt includes the real value of the central bank's liabilities. The manner in which the central bank controls aggregate demand in a neutral fiscal environment is discussed. There is also an analysis of how the bank can provide the economy with an optimal supply of liquidity. It is shown that the government can follow whatever fiscal policy it wishes—one of neutrality or one to achieve some

---

a tax policy which treats the different kinds of investment alike will lead to too little investment of the kind which gives off external returns *relative* to other kinds of investment.

growth target—and use monetary policy to achieve whatever price trend it desires, at the same time optimizing the amount of liquidity by means of a third policy weapon, namely, the device of paying interest on money.

The final chapter presents a critique of neutralism. (The reader can go directly to this chapter without losing the main thread of the book.) The questions considered there are the following: Under what conditions would a neutral policy toward growth be Pareto-optimal from the standpoint of the present generation? What are the principal market imperfections and externalities which make it unlikely that a neutral policy would be optimal? How should these imperfections and externalities alter fiscal policy toward growth? Why may a neutral fiscal policy be inferior to one with smaller taxes when generations overlap? And finally, even if a neutral policy (or some other policy) should produce a growth path which is optimal from the standpoint of the present generation, is such optimality an ethical standard for government policy?

Chapter 2

Fiscal neutrality

toward growth

in a barter economy

The subject of this chapter is the nature of neutral tax policy in a simple barter economy. Later, fiscal neutrality in an efficient monetary economy will be analyzed. Our study begins with consideration of an economy lacking government expenditures on goods and services. A government sector which provides public consumption and public investments will be introduced subsequently.

2.1 Neutrality without Government Expenditure

We shall investigate neutral tax policy in the context of a simple neo-classical model. The main features of that model are recalled in the section which follows.

2.1.1 The setting

Suppose that production takes place periodically. Let K_t denote the stock of capital on hand at the beginning of the tth period. This stock of goods may be either consumed or invested. Let C_t denote the amount consumed. Then the rest, $K_t - C_t$, can be combined with the available labor supply L_t and the available "land" supply N_t to produce—for availability next period—a new crop of capital K_{t+1}.

We suppose that production takes place according to a smooth, neoclassical production function which exhibits constant returns to scale and is such that marginal products are everywhere positive and diminishing.

We suppose also that there is pure competition in commodity and factor markets (including a perfect credit market) and that there are no externalities in production among firms. In each period, therefore, profit-maximizing firms will hire labor and land up to the points where their marginal productivities (suitably discounted) equal, respectively, the wage rate w_t and rental rate v_t. For simplicity we shall suppose the supplies of labor and land to be constant over time. Hence, the earnings of both these factors will be called *rents*. Their total earnings in period t—total rents—will be denoted R_t.

A firm will invest capital up to the point where its net marginal productivity is equal to the rate of interest. The single-period rate of interest in period t (the interest rate on loans made at the beginning of t and due at the beginning of $t + 1$) will be denoted r_{t+1}. It can be shown that capital invested $K_t - C_t$ plus total rent R_t must equal total output discounted by this rate of interest, $K_{t+1}/(1 + r_{t+1})$.*

---

* The foregoing can be expressed mathematically as follows: The production function

$$K_{t+1} = F(K_t - C_t, L_t, N_t; t)$$

which may shift from period to period, has the properties

$$\frac{\partial F}{\partial K_t}, \frac{\partial F}{\partial L_t}, \frac{\partial F}{\partial N_t} > 0$$

$$\frac{\partial^2 F}{\partial K_t^2}, \frac{\partial^2 F}{\partial L_t^2}, \frac{\partial^2 F}{\partial N_t^2} < 0$$

and $$\frac{\partial F}{\partial K}(K_t - C_t) + \frac{\partial F}{\partial L_t}L_t + \frac{\partial F}{\partial N_t}N_t = K_{t+1}$$

for all K_t, C_t, L_t, N_t, and t (time).

The rate of interest in period t satisfies the relation

$$r_{t+1} = \frac{\partial F}{\partial K_t} - 1$$

and the wage rate and rental rate satisfy the relations

To simplify the analysis, we shall suppose that the population is constant and expects to live forever. In the first period (period zero), therefore, the population starts with a given capital stock, $K_0 = K_o$ of which it consumes C_0, investing the rest to produce K_1, of which it consumes C_1, and so on. Hence the population will plan an infinite sequence of consumption $(C_0, C_1, C_2, \ldots)$.

In order to conduct the analysis on an aggregative level, we shall suppose that the aggregate of the consumption programs planned by the members of the community behaves as if it were chosen to maximize a community utility function subject to an aggregate net-worth constraint. Thus the community chooses in the first period that first-period consumption C_0 which maximizes community utility subject to the restraint that the present discounted value of the planned (aggregate) consumption program equal the community's expected net worth (after taxes) in the first period, say W_0^e:

$$C_0 + \frac{C_1}{1 + r_1} + \frac{C_2}{(1 + r_1)(1 + r_2^e)} + \cdots = W_0^e$$

where r_t^e denotes the interest rate expected to prevail between period $t - 1$ and t.*

$$w_t = \frac{\partial F / \partial L_t}{1 + r_{t+1}} \qquad v_t = \frac{\partial F / \partial N_t}{1 + r_{t+1}}$$

Since $R_t = w_t L + v_t N$,

$$R_t = \frac{(\partial F / \partial L_t)L_t}{1 + r_t} + \frac{(\partial F / \partial N_t)N_t}{1 + r_t}$$

and, from the last condition on the production function,

$$K_t - C_t + R_t = \frac{K_{t+1}}{1 + r_{t+1}}$$

* Samuelson has shown for the case of a finite number of goods that social indifference curves (contours of a social utility function) exist if individual indifference curves exist and the government redistributes wealth (by lump-sum taxes and transfers) among individuals so as to maximize a social welfare function. To ensure the existence of individual indifference curves here (where we have an infinite number of consumptions), we shall postulate *time preference*. See Paul A. Samuelson, "Social Indifference Curves," *Quarterly Journal of Economics*, vol. 70 (February, 1956), pp. 1–22.

More recently, Negishi demonstrated that these social indifference curves are convex if the individual indifference curves are convex and if the social welfare function is quasi-concave. See Takashi Negishi, "On Social Welfare Function," *Quarterly Journal of Economics*, vol. 77 (February, 1963), pp. 156–158.

If government debt and net taxes (taxes net of transfer payments by the government) are equal to zero, then

$$W_0^e = K_o + R_0 + \frac{R_1^e}{1 + r_1} + \frac{R_2^e}{(1 + r_1)(1 + r_2^e)} + \cdots$$

where R_0, already defined, is the total rent earned by land and labor in the first period and R_t^e is the rent expected to be earned in period t. Note that if expectations of rents and interest rates are in error, then the present value of the sequence of consumptions which will actually be chosen may exceed or fall short of the present value of the consumption program planned in the first period. This discrepancy will be especially likely if taxes and government debt, which also figure in expected net worth, are set adventitiously.

Now we introduce government debt and taxation. Let S_o denote the size of the interest payments (due at the beginning of each period) necessary to "service" the government debt existing at the beginning of the first period, i.e., the debt arising from past borrowing. The equilibrium market value of this initial debt depends upon its maturity and interest-rate expectations. Suppose for simplicity that all the initial debt matures after n periods, $n \geq 1$. Then its equilibrium value *ex interest* (after interest due the beginning of the first period has been paid), to be denoted B_0, is

$$B_0 = S_o \left[\frac{1}{1 + r_1} + \frac{1}{(1 + r_1)(1 + r_2^e)} + \cdots + \frac{1}{(1 + r_1) \cdots (1 + r_n^e)} \right] + \frac{P_o}{(1 + r_1) \cdots (1 + r_n^e)}$$

where P_o is the principal borrowed by the government to be repaid at the maturation of the initial debt. The total addition to expected net worth made by the debt is $S_o + B_0$, which is the first interest payment plus the value of the debt ex interest.

Concerning taxation, we restrict our analysis to taxes of the lump-sum variety. As we demonstrate below, neutral fiscal policy is not generally possible when taxes are levied on income or expenditure. In any case the distortions of economic decisions arising from the substitution effects of income, excise, and other taxes not of the lump-sum type are secondary to the fact that the level of taxes of whatever kind—the size of the budgetary surplus or deficit—may cause the economy to depart from the neutral equilibrium.

Let T_0 denote the level in the first period of taxes, net of non-interest transfers. (We do not deduct S_o from gross taxes to obtain T_0.) Let T_t^e denote the net taxes expected (in the first period) by the community to be levied in period t. The present discounted value V_0^e of these expected future taxes is

$$V_0^e = \frac{T_1^e}{1 + r_1} + \frac{T_2^e}{(1 + r_1)(1 + r_2^e)} + \cdots$$
$$+ \frac{T_t^e}{(1 + r_1) \cdots (1 + r_t^e)} + \cdots$$

Taxes and expected future taxes reduce expected net worth by $T_0 + V_0^e$.

For economy of notation let Z_0^e denote the present discounted value of future rents

$$Z_0^e = \frac{R_1^e}{1 + r_1} + \frac{R_2^e}{(1 + r_1)(1 + r_2^e)} + \cdots$$
$$+ \frac{R_e^t}{(1 + r_1) \cdots (1 + r_t^e)} + \cdots$$

Then expected net worth is

$$W_0^e = K_o + R_0 + Z_0^e + B_0 + S_o - T_0 - V_0^e$$

when taxes and government debt are present.

Since there are no government expenditures on goods and services, the difference $S_o - T_0$ is the budgetary deficit in the first period.[1] If positive, this deficit must be financed by the sale of new government debt (supposing there to be no public capital available for the government to disinvest); if negative, by the purchase of debt. Hence, the

---

[1] Of course, T_0 measures "algebraic" net taxes and may be positive or negative. Similarly, the algebraic deficit $S_o - T_0$ may be negative—a budgetary surplus. Any surplus the government receives must be "lent," since we are not allowing the government to purchase or to stock goods. "Lending" may take the form of retiring the initial public debt or of actual lending to the private sector. If the government should be a net creditor, S_o and B_0 will be negative. If this interest earned by government is returned to the taxpayers rather than lent (which it need not be), the transfer reduces net taxes by that amount. Then a "balanced" budget (meaning algebraic taxes only to pay algebraic interest owed by government) implies $T_0 = S_o < 0$.

equilibrium value of the final public debt in the first period (the initial debt plus the first-period change of the debt) is equal to $B_0 + S_o - T_0$. It will be convenient to define

$$D_0^e = B_0 + S_o - T_0 - V_0^e$$

which we shall call the *effective government debt*. Then the foregoing states that the community chooses the consumption level of the first period, C_0, as an element of a planned consumption program whose present discounted value is equal to[1]

$$W_0^e = K_o + R_0 + Z_0^e + D_0^e$$

We can depict the first-period equilibrium diagrammatically, as in Figure 1, if we view the community's decision in the first period as the selection of a pair (C_0, W_1^e) subject to the constraint

$$C_0 + \frac{W_1^e}{1 + r_1} = W_0^e$$

where $W_1^e = K_1 + (1 + r_1)Z_0^e + (1 + r_1)D_0^e$ denotes expected wealth next period. The reader need not study this diagram to understand the analysis that follows. If the members of the community were to plan to consume nothing, they would expect wealth next period equal to $W_0^e(1 + r_1)$; if they were to plan to consume all their wealth (although collectively they could consume only K_o), they would expect wealth next period to be zero. Taking W_0^e and r_1 as fixed at their equilibrium values, this *budget constraint* on consumers can be represented by the straight line AA in Figure 1.

Continuing to take as fixed the future interest-rate and future rent expectations corresponding to the given equilibrium, one can also derive a community (or social) indifference map in the (C_0, W_1^e) plane from the basic indifference relations (among the consumptions of the various periods). Consumers will choose the point on the budget line which lies on the highest indifference curve. This point is at E, where AA is tangent to the indifference curve UU.

[1] Note that the planned consumption sequence will turn out to be the one which is optimal (among all feasible sequences) only if W_0^e equals the present value of the latter (preferred) program *and* all future interest rates are correctly foreseen. The consumption program planned on the basis of W_0^e and the sequence $\{r_t^e\}$ may be infeasible or may be improved upon.

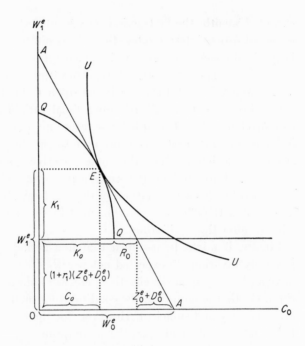

Figure 1   **Equilibrium in the First Period**

Because the economy is efficient—it produces the greatest K_1 for given K_o, C_0, L, and N—this equilibrium point must also lie on the transformation curve QQ, which indicates how maximum K_1 is a function of C_0, given K_o, L, and N. And since (by virtue of pure competition) the rate of interest equals the net marginal productivity of capital, the slope of the budget line, $-(1 + r_1)$, must equal the slope of the transformation curve at E, which is $\partial K_1/\partial C_0$. Hence the equilibrium is also a point of tangency of the budget line with the transformation curve.[1]

The above formulation of consumption decisions implies that consumption in the first period is a function of equilibrium first-period

[1] The diagram cannot legitimately be used as a device for comparative statical analysis—for analyzing the effect upon the solution of changes in the state variables K_o, S_o, P_o or of changes in the policy variable T_0. Such changes might alter expectations of future rents and interest rates and thus both alter $Z_0{}^e$ and shift the indifference-curve map.

expected wealth, the first-period rate of interest, and the sequence of expected future interest rates. But this is not helpful until something is specified concerning the way in which expectations are formed.

We shall suppose that expectations of future rents and interest rates are "rational," that they are based upon estimates of current and future investment, *not directly* upon fiscal variables which, therefore, can affect future rents and interest rates only indirectly through their influence upon current and future investment. In particular two fiscal situations which produce the same effective government debt will be supposed to produce the same expectations of future rents and interest rates. Hence, variations of the fiscal variables S_o, P_o, T_0 which do not alter the effective government debt (at given rates of interest) will not alter the equilibrium.

Finally, it might be assumed that first-period consumption is not generally invariant to expected net worth—that fiscal changes which have an impact upon the effective debt will indeed change the equilibrium. On that assumption, the conditions for neutrality derived below are necessary and sufficient. However, for the most part, the analysis below does not depend upon this assumption.

The consumption possibilities, preferences, and market behavior of the model when government expenditures are absent have now been described. In the next section we define a neutral fiscal policy and derive the formal conditions for neutrality of the tax level. In subsequent sections we characterize the budgetary policies which satisfy these conditions.

2.1.2 Formal conditions for fiscal neutrality

When there are no government expenditures, we shall say that fiscal neutrality exists *by definition* if the government has no liabilities to the public and is not expected to contract any (by future negative net taxes) and if the public has no net tax liabilities to the government and does not expect to have any net tax liabilities in the future. In short, neutrality toward growth prevails by definition if—apart from the government's redistribution of wealth by positive and negative taxes which add up to zero—the government is virtually absent. In terms of our notation, neutrality exists by definition if

$$S_o = B_0 = T_0 = T_1^e = \cdots = T_t^e = \cdots = 0$$

While the above condition is sufficient for neutrality, it is not necessary. We shall say that another fiscal policy is also neutral if it produces the same equilibrium—hence the same amount of consumption in the first period—as would be produced if the government were neutral by definition. In other words, the consumption-investment mix chosen by the market when the above condition is satisfied is the basis for deciding whether or not a specified combination of S_o, B_0, T_0, etc., is neutral: it is so if and only if the same mix is chosen by the market. Notice that as a consequence of this definition fiscal policy would be neutral in our sense—indeed, unavoidably so—if for some reason the government's debt and taxes were "neutral" in the frequently used sense that variations of the government's debt and taxes could have no effect upon the equilibrium configuration of interest rate, consumption, and so on.[1] We shall revert to this point below.

Our task in this section is to determine the conditions on S_o, B_0, T_0 and $V_0{}^e$ for neutrality. What combinations of these variables will cause consumption to be the same as in the equilibrium which occurs when there is neutrality by definition?

Consider the first-period equilibrium (assumed to be unique) when neutrality exists by definition. Let $\hat{C}_0$ and $\hat{K}_1$ denote first-period consumption and next-period capital, respectively. Let $\hat{R}_0$ denote the total rents in this equilibrium, and let $\hat{r}_1$ denote the equilibrium first-period rate of interest. Associated with this equilibrium is also a sequence of expected future interest rates $\hat{r}_2{}^e$, $\hat{r}_3{}^e$, . . . and future rents $\hat{R}_2{}^e$, $\hat{R}_3{}^e$; denote by $\hat{Z}_0{}^e$ the associated value of $Z_0{}^e$. Since $D_0{}^e$ is equal to zero in this situation, the value of expected net worth corresponding to this equilibrium, denoted $\hat{W}_0{}^e$, is

$$\hat{W}_0{}^e = K_o + \hat{R}_0 + \hat{Z}_0{}^e$$

Consider now any combination of values, not necessarily zero, of the fiscal variables S_o, P_o, T_0, etc. If these values make $D_0{}^e$ equal to zero when evaluated at the interest rates $\hat{r}_1$, $\hat{r}_2{}^e$, . . . , then $(\hat{C}_0,\hat{K}_1)$ remains the equilibrium. For, as supposed above, those combinations of

---

[1] The word "neutral" here is used in the strong sense in which money is often said to be neutral when its size has no effect upon the rate of interest, hence upon consumption, real money holdings, etc. We shall always use quotation marks around the term when employed in this strong sense.

values of the fiscal variables which produce the same value of $D_0{}^e$, evaluated at interest rates which are equilibrium rates for one of these combinations, produce the same equilibrium. Hence all those values of the fiscal variables which keep $D_0{}^e = 0$, when evaluated at $\hat{r}_1$, $\hat{r}_2{}^e$, . . . , produce the same value of expected net worth, namely $\widehat{W}_0{}^e$, and hence the same equilibrium $(\hat{C}_0, \hat{K}_1)$. Therefore the tax policy which makes effective government debt equal to zero is said to be neutral. Our formal condition for neutrality is that $D_0{}^e = 0$.*

2.1.3 Characterizing neutral policy when no initial debt

When $S_o = P_o = 0$, we have[1]

$$D_0{}^e = - T_0 - V_0{}^e$$

Hence the tax level is neutral if

$$- T_0 = V_0{}^e$$

If $V_0{}^e$ is a constant, independent of T_0, then the size of the algebraic deficit, $- T_0$, is neutral when it equals this constant (which might be positive or negative) and this fully characterizes a neutral policy. If $V_0{}^e$ is a function of the first-period tax level (or deficit), then more interesting results can be obtained.

One hypothesis concerning $V_0{}^e$, a hypothesis put forward most recently by Martin Bailey, states that the present discounted value of the future taxes expected by taxpayers will always equal the value of the interest-bearing debt issued (currently and in the past) by the government.[2] When there is no initial debt, this means that $V_0{}^e$ is equal to $- T_0$, the algebraic deficit of the first period.

Taxpayers will have this expectation if, for example, they believe that after some point in the future the budget will be regularly bal-

---

* If more than one value of $D_0{}^e$ can produce the equilibrium $(\hat{C}_0, \hat{K}_1)$, then the tax levels which produce these other values of $D_0{}^e$ must also be said to be neutral. In this case the condition that $D_0{}^e = 0$ is sufficient but not necessary for neutrality.

[1] It should be understood that present discounted values like $V_0{}^e$ are to be evaluated at the interest rates corresponding to the neutral equilibrium, namely, $\hat{r}_1$, $\hat{r}_2{}^e$, . . . , for it is at those interest rates that $D_0{}^e = 0$ produces the neutral equilibrium $(\hat{C}_0, \hat{K}_1)$.

[2] Martin J. Bailey, *National Income and the Price Level* (New York: McGraw-Hill Book Company, 1962), pp. 75–77, 81.

anced. In that event, any debt outstanding at the moment of shift to a balanced-budget policy must be serviced by a level of taxes higher than would be necessary if there were no debt. If the government is a net creditor at the onset of the balanced-budget policy, the interest earned by the government on the negative algebraic debt of that time will be transferred to taxpayers in the form of tax reductions or increases in transfers, hence a reduction of net taxes. A deficit (surplus) in the present would necessitate future net tax increases (reductions) whose present discounted value would just equal the present deficit (surplus). This is only one, but perhaps the most plausible, rationale for the hypothesis. We return to the possible basis for such expectations in section 2.1.8.

On this hypothesis any tax level is neutral: $V_0^e = -T_0$ for all values of T_0. Taxpayers will regard a government surplus as an act of saving on its behalf, and a government deficit as dissaving. Personal saving will increase (decrease) by the amount of the deficit (surplus); consumption will remain unchanged. In these circumstances tax policy is *intrinsically neutral*: it is incapable of changing the equilibrium level of consumption from the neutral level $\hat{C}_0$.

While we shall give this hypothesis its due, let us turn now to a more orthodox hypothesis, which states that the (algebraic) debt created by the first-period (algebraic) deficit, namely $-T_0$ (since $S_o = B_0 = 0$), is offset *incompletely if at all* by the expectation it induces of future taxes. More precisely, the hypothesis states that V_0^e is a continuous function of $-T_0$, with the property that $V_0^e/(-T_0) < 1$ for all $T_0 \neq 0$; it follows that $V_0^e = 0$ if $T_0 = 0$.

On this latter hypothesis, $-D_0^e = T_0 + V_0^e \gtreqless 0$ according as $T_0 \gtreqless 0$. V_0^e cannot fully offset the effect of T_0 on the sum $T_0 + V_0^e$. Hence, to induce $V_0^e = -T_0$, it is necessary and sufficient to equate T_0 to zero. A balanced budget, $T_0 = S_o = 0$, is therefore neutral. A deficit, $T_0 < S_o = 0$, will make $D_0^e > 0$, while a surplus, $T_0 > S_c = 0$, will make $D_0^e < 0$. The former will presumably produce a positive wealth effect upon consumption demand, causing $C_0 > \hat{C}_0$, while the latter will presumably produce a negative wealth effect upon consumption, causing $C_0 < \hat{C}_0$. For this reason an unbalanced-budget policy is not generally neutral when there is no initial debt.

2.1.4 "Neutralizing" the initial debt by lump-sum taxes

When S_o and P_o are not zero, the neutrality condition $D_0{}^e = 0$ can be written

$$B_0 + S_o - T_0 = V_0{}^e$$

In the previous section we first considered the hypothesis that taxpayers will form expectations of future taxes in such a way that $V_0{}^e$ is equal to whatever postdeficit debt, $B_0 + S_o - T_0$, the government produces by its choice of $T_0 - S_o$, the algebraic deficit of the first period. On this hypothesis, both the initial debt and the current deficit are intrinsically neutral: the effective government debt will be zero whatever the values of B_0, S_o, and T_0 since $V_0{}^e$ will always offset them.

The second hypothesis considered states that $V_0{}^e$ is a function of the (postdeficit) debt. When $S_o = P_o = B_0 = 0$, this debt was just $-T_0$. In the present case the postdeficit debt is $B_0 + S_o - T_0$. Hence, this second hypothesis states that $V_0{}^e = \varphi(B_0 + S_o - T_0)$ with the properties that $\varphi(0) = 0$ and that $V_0{}^e/(B_0 + S_o - T_0) < 1$ for all

$$B_0 + S_o - T_0 \neq 0$$

This means that the present discounted value of expected future taxes is always smaller than the postdeficit government debt if the latter is greater than zero.[1]

On this hypothesis, $D_0{}^e = 0$ if and only if $B_0 + S_o - T_0 = 0$ just as, in the previous section when $B_0 = S_o = 0$, $-T_0 = 0$ was required for $D_0{}^e = 0$. This is shown in Figure 2: $V_0{}^e$ intersects the 45° line so as to make $V_0{}^e = B_0 + S_o - T_0$ only at the origin, where $B_0 + S_o - T_0 = V_0{}^e = 0$.

The result implies that the initial government debt must be retired in the first period if the effective government debt is to be zero. For if a nonzero algebraic debt is left outstanding $(B_0 + S_o - T_0 \neq 0)$, it produces a nonzero effective debt $(D_0{}^e \neq 0)$. Fiscal neutrality requires that all initial debt be immediately retired on the above hypothesis that government debt is only incompletely offset by expectation of future taxes in consumers' estimations of their net worth.

----

[1] If the algebraic debt is negative, the hypothesis means that the present discounted value of expected future transfers is smaller than the government's holdings of assets (its negative debt).

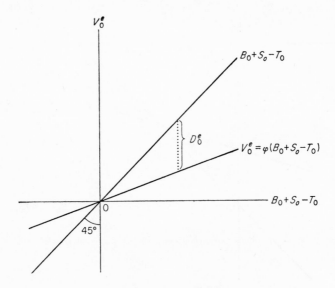

Figure 2   **Determination of the Neutral Tax Level**

If this result is not entirely plausible, it is perhaps because the hypothesis is not realistic. Let us consider the new hypothesis (the third of our hypotheses) that expected future taxes depend not only on current government debt but upon the current tax level as well, for taxpayers tend to extrapolate the current tax level into the future. Precisely, we shall hypothesize that $V_0^e = \Phi(B_0 + S_o - T_0, T_0)$ and that the function has the properties $\Phi(0,0) = 0$, $0 \leq \Phi_1 < 1$, and $\Phi_2 > 0$.*

In other words, $V_0^e = 0$ if there is no debt and zero net taxes; a rise of the debt, taxes constant, is offset incompletely (if at all) by a rise of expected future taxes; and a rise of the first-period net tax level, holding the debt constant, induces a rise in expected future taxes. Then $dV_0^e/dT_0 = -\Phi_1 + \Phi_2 > -1$, or equivalently

$$\frac{dV_0^e}{d(-T_0)} = \Phi_1 - \Phi_2 < 1$$

* Φ_1 signifies $\partial V_0^e/\partial(B_0 + S_o - T_0)$, the partial derivative of V_0^e with respect to the postdeficit debt, i.e., the change of V_0^e per unit change of the debt, holding T_0 constant. Similarly, Φ_2 signifies $\partial V_0^e/\partial T_0$.

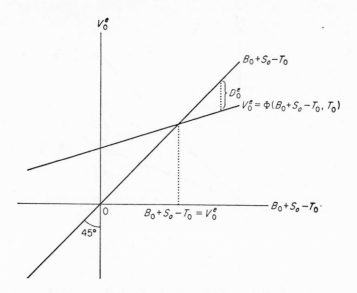

Figure 3 **Determination of the Neutral Tax Level**

which is to say that a tax reduction (which raises the first-period deficit, $S_o - T_0$) is offset incompletely (if at all) in its impact upon $D_0{}^e$ by any rise of $V_0{}^e$ which it may induce. (Hence taxation is not "neutral" in the sense of having no impact upon the effective government debt and thus the equilibrium.)

On this third hypothesis about future tax expectations, the total retirement of a positive initial debt,[1] meaning $T_0 = S_o + B_0 > 0$, would cause $D_0{}^e < 0$ since $\Phi(0, T_0) > 0$ for all $T_0 > 0$. A zero net tax $T_0 = 0$ would cause $D_0{}^e > 0$ since $\Phi(B_0 + S_o, 0) < B_0 + S_o$ for all $B_0 + S_o > 0$. Hence, if the initial algebraic debt is positive, $D_0{}^e = 0$ requires a positive posttax debt, $B_0 + S_o - T_0$, and a positive tax. Similar findings are obtained, *mutatis mutandis*, if the initial algebraic debt is negative. The solution for a positive initial debt is shown in Figure 3, where Φ is depicted as a linear function.

---

[1] By a positive initial algebraic debt we mean $B_0 > 0$. The discussion above assumes that P_o and S_o have the same algebraic sign and that $r_t{}^e > 0$ for all t so that S_o and B_0 have the same algebraic sign.

2.1.5 Does debt neutralization require a tax increase exceeding the debt service?

Thus we see that neutrality does not require total retirement of the initial debt if taxpayers tend to extrapolate to a degree their present taxes ($\Phi_2 > 0$). The initial debt can be neutralized by a more modest tax level. But we have not investigated the relation between the neutralizing tax level and S_o. Would the tax increase necessary to neutralize the debt make the algebraic budgetary surplus, $T_0 - S_o$, positive, zero, or negative? That is, would neutrality, in the presence of a positive initial debt, put the "budget" in surplus, in balance, or in deficit?

We found, on our second hypothesis, that a balanced budget, given a positive initial debt, would have created a positive effective debt. This second hypothesis differs from the third only in respect to Φ_2 o the Φ function: it makes $\Phi_2 = 0$, which is to say there is no extrapolation of present taxes. It should be clear, therefore, that a balanced budget might also be nonneutral on the third hypothesis. For if the present net tax level (given the debt) has a sufficiently small effect upon V_0^e, meaning that Φ_2 is sufficiently small, then net taxes will have to exceed the debt service to neutralize the initial debt.

There are, however, special cases in which a balanced budget will be exactly neutral despite the presence of nonzero government debt. Suppose that $T_t^e = T_0$ for all $t \geq 1$. (This implies $\Phi_1 = 0$; that is, the level of the debt, net taxes constant, has no effect upon future tax expectations.) Then

$$V_0^e = T_0 \left[\frac{1}{1 + r_1} + \frac{1}{(1 + r_1)(1 + r_2^e)} + \cdots \right]$$

Now if the initial debt is entirely in consols, then

$$B_0 = S_o \left[\frac{1}{1 + r_1} + \frac{1}{(1 + r_1)(1 + r_2^e)} + \cdots \right]$$

so that $D_0^e = 0$ if and only if $T_0 = S_o$.

If the entire initial debt matures after n periods, then the formula for B_0 can be expressed as follows:

$$B_0 = S_o \left[\frac{1}{1 + r_1} + \frac{1}{(1 + r_1)(1 + r_2{}^e)} + \cdots \right]$$

$$+ \frac{P_o}{(1 + r_1) \cdots (1 + r_n{}^e)}$$

$$\left\{ 1 - \frac{S_o}{P_o} \left[\frac{1}{1 + r_{n+1}^e} + \frac{1}{(1 + r_{n+1}^e)(1 + r_{n+2}^e)} + \cdots \right] \right\}$$

Hence $\quad B_0 = S_o \left[\dfrac{1}{1 + r_1} + \dfrac{1}{(1 + r_1)(1 + r_2{}^e)} + \cdots \right]$

if and only if

$$S_o \left[\frac{1}{1 + r_{n+1}^e} + \frac{1}{(1 + r_{n+1}^e)(1 + r_{n+2}^e)} + \cdots \right] = P_o$$

in which case $T_0 = S_o$ again satisfies $D_0{}^e = 0$.*

Clearly $T_0 \gtreqless S_o$ for $D_0{}^e = 0$ according as

$$S_o \left[\frac{1}{1 + r_{n+1}^e} + \frac{1}{(1 + r_{n+1}^e)(1 + r_{n+2}^e)} + \cdots \right] \lesseqgtr P_o$$

Hence a balanced budget could be neutral, though of course it need not be. $T_0 < S_o$ might be necessary for $D_0{}^e = 0$. If the existing debt is less than consols would be worth which paid the same aggregate S_o, then $V_0{}^e > B_0$ when $T_0 = S_o$. Since $dD_0{}^e/dT_0 < -1$, $D_0{}^e = 0$ requires $T_0 < S_o$, that is, the issue of additional debt.[1,2]

---

* The bonds will sell at "par," $B_0 = P_o$, on the condition that

$$S_o \left[\frac{1}{1 + r_1} + \frac{1}{(1 + r_1)(1 + r_2{}^e)} + \cdots + \frac{1}{(1 + r_1) \cdots (1 + r_n{}^e)} \right]$$

$$= P_o \left[1 - \frac{1}{(1 + r_1) \cdots (1 + r_n{}^e)} \right]$$

This condition depends upon interest rates over the next n periods, while the condition in the text depends upon the interest rates after n periods; thus they are not equivalent. However, if $r_t{}^e = \bar{r}$ for all t, they do become identical. Then the condition in the text becomes $S_o(1/\bar{r}) = P_o$. And the par condition can be written

$$S_o \left[\frac{1}{\bar{r}} - \frac{1}{(1 + \bar{r})^n} \frac{1}{\bar{r}} \right] = P_o \left[1 - \frac{1}{(1 + \bar{r})^n} \right]$$

Hence
$$\frac{S_o}{P_o} = \frac{1 - (1 + \bar{r})^{-n}}{(1/\bar{r})[1 - (1 + \bar{r})^{-n}]} = \bar{r}$$

[1] However, if expectations are borne out (which may not be feasible under a nonneutral policy but may be feasible under a neutral policy), the policy will

A balanced budget would be neutral in general only if the Φ function satisfied the condition $B_0 = \Phi(B_0, S_o)$ for all S_o, P_o, and n (maturity). There is no evident rationale for such a condition.

This condition is to be distinguished from the stronger condition $\Phi(B_0 + S_o - T_0, T_0) = B_0 + S_o - T_0$ for all T_0. This is the meaning of the first hypothesis considered. On this condition every tax level, including $T_0 = S_o$, is neutral. Our third hypothesis excluded this possibility by the assumption that $dV_0^e/dT_0 = -\Phi_1 + \Phi_2 > -1$.

2.1.6 Neutrality not generally feasible if taxes are not lump-sum

In the above analysis of how the debt may be neutralized by lump-sum taxes, we supposed that the supply of labor (equivalently, the demand for leisure) is independent of the wage rate and expected net worth. Our results do not require this.

Suppose that the supply of labor in the first period, L_0, is a function of the wage rate w_0 and expected net worth,

$$L_0 = J(w_0, W_0^e)$$

Now a change of the wage rate will have a substitution effect and a wealth (or capitalized-income) effect. If we fix W_0^e, however, the wage-rate change will have only a substitution effect. Therefore we may take $\partial L_0/\partial w_0$ to be positive: given net worth, a rise of the wage rate increases labor supply. Also, an increase of net worth increases leisure: $\partial L_0/\partial W_0^e > 0$.

In addition, we have the consumption-demand function which has been implicit in the previous analysis,

$$C_0 = C(r_1, r_2^e, r_3^e, \ldots, W_0^e)$$

---

switch after n periods to surpluses equal in present discounted value to the present value of the interim deficits of the first n periods. This follows immediately from the condition $D_0^e = 0$.

[2] It might be thought that if the present generation expects to live for only a finite time N, then V_0^e is the present value of a truncated sequence of T_t^e, $1 \leq t \leq N$, so that there is a presumption that a surplus is required to neutralize the debt. But whether or not this is so depends upon how the present generation takes account of the expected tax liabilities of future generations, which include the present generation's heirs, heirs' heirs, etc.

Again, an increase in the first-period rate of interest, given net worth and future expected interest rates, must be supposed to decrease consumption (increase saving), there being only a substitution effect when net worth is held constant. Hence $\partial C_0/\partial r_1 < 0$. Also, $\partial C_0/\partial W_0^e > 0$.*

Finally, let $\hat{w}_0$, $\hat{L}_0$, and $\hat{C}_0$ denote values of the wage rate, labor supply, and consumption in neutral equilibrium.

Suppose that the economy is initially in neutral equilibrium, with no debt and taxes. Hence $W_0^e = \hat{W}_0^e$, $D_0^e = 0$. Imagine now that a unit of government debt is injected into this economy: $B_0 + S_o = 1$. At the initial (neutral) rates of interest and wage rate, expected net worth would then exceed its neutral level by one unit: $W_0^e = \hat{W}_0^e + 1$, $D_0^e = 1$. This will normally stimulate consumption and leisure beyond their neutral levels: $C_0 > \hat{C}_0$, $L_0 < \hat{L}_0$. But by levying the appropriate amount of net lump-sum taxes the government can raise present plus expected future taxes so as to make $T_0 + V_0^e = 1$, $D_0^e = 0$, and $W_0^e = \hat{W}_0^e$ and thus neutralize the incidence of the debt. For if expected net worth is restored to its neutral level, then the supply of labor and consumption demand will return to their neutral equilibrium values. The neutralization is possible because the tax has only a wealth (or net-worth) effect upon consumption demand and labor supply. The same tax which neutralizes the impact of the debt upon consumption demand will also neutralize the impact of the debt upon labor supply.

The situation is different if taxes are not lump-sum. Suppose, for example, that the government attempts to neutralize the debt by means of an "expenditure" (or consumption) tax, one that is expected to remain in force. Suppose that the tax is proportional to consumption, and let τ denote the proportional tax rate.

Under this tax the rate of interest will continue to equal the marginal productivity of capital since the terms at which a unit of future consumption can be purchased by a reduction of present consumption are unaffected by the expenditure tax; the expenditure tax is not a tax on saving. Similarly, the market wage rate will continue to equate the

---

* The labor-supply and consumption-demand functions can be interpreted as coming out of the maximization of utility as a function of the sequence of consumption and sequence of leisure chosen by the community subject to a budget constraint.

marginal productivity of labor. But labor supply will be a function, not of the market wage rate, but rather of the terms at which a unit of consumption can be purchased by the reduction of leisure (the increase of labor). These "terms" will be increased by the tax since $1 + \tau$ units of wealth (or wage income) must be surrendered to obtain one unit of consumption. Hence, the "wage rate" in terms of consumption will be $w_0/(1 + \tau)$ rather than w_0 after the tax,

$$L_0 = J\left(\frac{w_0}{1 + \tau}, W_0^e\right)$$

It follows that the expenditure tax cannot simultaneously neutralize the impacts of the debt on both consumption demand and labor supply. To neutralize the impact of the debt upon consumption demand alone, it is necessary to restore expected net worth to the neutral level, $\hat{W}_0^e$, by setting τ so as to make $D_0^e = 0$. But if $W_0^e = \hat{W}_0^e$, the impact of the debt on the labor supply will be *not* be neutralized. For if $W_0^e = \hat{W}_0^e$ and $w_0 = \hat{w}_0$ (which must be the case if $L_0 = \hat{L}_0$ and $C_0 = \hat{C}_0$, that is, if both consumption and labor supply are restored to their neutral levels), then $w_0/(1 + \tau) = \hat{w}_0/(1 + \tau)$, which is *smaller* than $\hat{w}_0$, the wage rate in terms of consumption before the tax. This fall of the relevant after-tax rate will decrease labor supply. Hence, if the impact of the debt on consumption demand is neutralized, the impact of the debt on labor supply cannot be. As a consequence of the debt, either $L_0 < \hat{L}_0$ or $C_0 > \hat{C}_0$, or both, when an expenditure tax is used.[1]

A somewhat more complicated argument shows that an income tax cannot generally neutralize a government debt. The complication is that interest rates relevant to consumption demand, as well as the wage rate relevant to consumption demand, are affected by the income tax rate.

Let τ denote the proportional income tax rate, and suppose that

[1] Contrariwise, it is often said that an expenditure tax distorts labor-leisure decisions but not consumption-saving decisions. Apropos this notion one should be careful about assuming that the neutral equilibrium is optimal and hence should not be subjected to distortions. Second, it is only if the government elects to neutralize the impact of the debt upon consumption that the consumption-saving decision will not be distorted; in fact, the government could elect to neutralize the impact upon labor supply and thus allow consumption to bear the whole brunt of the debt.

this rate is expected to be permanent. Then the labor-supply function becomes

$$L_0 = J[w_0(1 - \tau), W_0^e]$$

and the consumption-demand function becomes

$$C_0 = C[r_1(1 - \tau), r_2^e(1 - \tau), \ldots, W_0^e]$$

A little reflection shows that to neutralize the impact of the debt on consumption demand alone it would be necessary to tax so as to make $W_0^e < \hat{W}_0^e$ in order to offset the (positive) impact upon consumption of the fall of after-tax interest rates brought about by the introduction of a positive τ. To neutralize the impact of the debt on labor supply alone it would also be necessary to cause $W_0^e < \hat{W}_0^e$ in order to offset the (negative) impact upon labor supply of the fall of after-tax wage rates brought about by the positive τ. But it will be an accident if the same tax rate which would neutralize the debt's impact upon consumption demand would also neutralize the debt's impact upon labor supply. Hence, it is not *generally* possible exactly to neutralize a positive initial government debt by means of an income tax.

The difference between our results for expenditure and income taxes is worth noting. The oft-alleged superiority of an expenditure tax over an income tax (on efficiency grounds) is not borne out by our analysis. Indeed, the income tax may be superior precisely because it produces substitution effects upon both labor supply and consumption demand rather than only on the former. But a full, rigorous analysis would take us beyond the scope of this volume.

2.1.7 A digression: Is a government debt a burden?

While much controversy surrounds the consequences of debts and deficits, it is widely held that a positive initial government debt imposes a "burden" on the economy. A debt may be said to impose a burden if it precludes some resource allocation which is superior to all allocations which are feasible given the debt.[1]

---

[1] This section asks how potential welfare depends upon the initial public debt, *given the initial capital stock.* Many writers have emphasized that the cumulative deficit of the past (giving rise to the present debt) reduces the welfare of the present generation by reducing the initial capital stock which is bequeathed to it. Modigliani, *op. cit.*, has ingeniously shown on certain assumptions that the size of the

The argument goes as follows: Lump-sum taxes by which the debt could be neutralized without an undesired effect on the distribution of income (or net worth) are not "feasible." The presence of a government debt makes desirable a rise of non-lump-sum tax rates; and this rise of tax rates blunts incentives to work and to save.

A lump-sum tax (or transfer) in the sense of a tax having no *substitution effect* but only a wealth or income effect is feasible only if the tax is believed by taxpayers to be nonrecurring or, if believed to be recurring, only if it is expected to recur in an amount which is independent of the taxpayer's income, expenditure, and wealth at all times in the future.[1] Hence a head tax, or poll tax, the tax being alike for all taxpayers, would qualify as a lump-sum tax. But such a tax would be unlikely to meet the government's income-distribution objectives. If the head tax varied among different people, there might be the suspicion that anyone earning additional income through a reduction of leisure or consumption would find himself having to pay a larger tax. It must be granted, therefore, that while extraordinary, once-for-all lump-sum taxes may be feasible, not all regular taxes, if they are to be satisfactory from the point of view of income distribution, can be effectively lump-sum.

Nevertheless, this conclusion leaves room for some use of head taxes. Suppose that the previous deficits (e.g., tax reductions) which produced the initial debt had caused an equal increment in every taxpayer's expected net worth. If the government was satisfied with the before-debt distribution of income, it might reasonably decide that to neutralize the debt it should levy an equal head tax on every taxpayer, thus causing an equal decrement in every taxpayer's net worth. Note that contrary to vulgar notions about the incidence of the debt, those who

---

initial debt measures the reduction of capital bequeathed. This effect on welfare might be called the *burden of deficits*, for that burden would remain if the initial public debt were repudiated or accidentally destroyed. But it would be better not to use such an emotive term as "burden" since a deficit need not be bad even on Modigliani's assumptions.

[1] There is an additional problem connected with a once-for-all lump-sum tax but not with a once-for-all lump-sum transfer: to achieve the desired effect on net worth, the tax may have to be so large as to require borrowing by many people to pay the tax. Imperfection of the capital market may make such borrowing expensive or even impossible.

presently hold the debt (e.g., the "rich") may not be those who bene-
fited from the tax reduction (or failure to raise taxes) which created
the debt (possibly the "rich" or possibly the "poor"). Hence the use of
head taxes to neutralize an initial debt cannot a priori be ruled
inequitable.

A once-for-all capital levy (wealth tax) may also be a feasible lump-
sum tax by means of which the debt can be neutralized. The virtue
of the capital levy over the head tax is that the tax can be made to vary
in the desired way with the wealth of the taxpayer. The tax will be
effectively lump-sum—i.e., have no substitution effects upon consumption and leisure—if the government can persuade the people that the
tax is not to be repeated in the future. The explanation that the tax
is occasioned by the debt and that the proceeds of the tax will permit
the retirement of the debt may help in this persuasion. But if people
expect deficits to occur in the future, they may expect a repetition of the
capital levy. However, the possibility that a capital levy will create
some positive expectation of its repetition in the minds of the taxpayers
does not weigh decisively against a capital levy: the magnitude by
which the capital levy would fail to neutralize the debt (because of these
substitution effects) must be compared with the magnitude by which
other kinds of taxes would fail.

Let us grant for the sake of argument that insofar as lump-sum taxes
exist which can neutralize the impact of the debt upon consumption and
leisure, these taxes are unsatisfactory from the point of view of their
effect upon income distribution. Does it then follow that with only
non-lump-sum taxes remaining, the debt is necessarily a burden?

Income distribution aside, this much is clear: If the impact of the
debt on consumption and leisure can be neutralized, then the debt
imposes no burden. As we argued in the preceding section, there is the
possibility that by accident an income tax rate can be found which will
neutralize a given debt. But it is not likely that every initial debt can be
neutralized by some income tax rate. (Note that if neutralization in our
sense is possible and if after-debt ownership of human and nonhuman
wealth is alike for every individual, then the neutralization will also be
neutral toward the distribution of wealth.[1])

---

[1] This possibility of full-scale neutralization we are unable to reconcile with
Meade's "proof" that the debt is a burden. Until it can be shown that neutraliza-

If the debt cannot be neutralized, we can conclude at least that the debt is burdensome *if* lump-sum transfers would not have been employed in the absence of an initial government debt. A debt is equivalent to the payment of lump-sum transfers to those holding the debt: it increases their expected net worth without having any substitution effects. Therefore, if it was not desirable to make any lump-sum transfer payments in the absence of a government debt, it cannot be desirable to have a government debt.

It is conceivable that an initial debt would be a boon rather than a burden. Suppose that the government would have liked to make certain lump-sum transfers to some or all of the population but found that any transfers made would have had substitution effects (for the reason explained above). Then, if the people to whom the government would have liked to give a lump-sum transfer happen to own government debt just equal to the desired transfer, the desired result would be attained. Hence, circumstances are conceivable in which an initial debt of some specification would be useful rather than burdensome.

It seems more likely that in actuality it is a negative debt that would be a boon and a positive debt a burden, because governments probably value the feasibility of lump-sum taxes more than the feasibility of lump-sum transfers. (If the government must levy positive net taxes on everyone, why should it prefer lump-sum transfers to reduction of non-lump-sum tax rates?) Since a negative debt is like a lump-sum tax—it decreases expected net worth without possessing any substitution effects—a negative debt might be a welcome substitute for (infeasible) desired lump-sum taxes.

In conclusion, the point to be emphasized is that presumably the debt can be neutralized approximately (if not exactly) by means of income taxation so that the burden of an initial debt, if it is burdensome, cannot be large when measured relative to the size of the debt. Further, even if the debt is burdensome, it does not follow that a current budgetary deficit would be bad policy. A deficit should be run if the economy would choose too small amounts of consumption and leisure by running a surplus. (As we pointed out in section 2.1.5,

tion is impossible, therefore, we reject Meade's argument. See J. E. Meade, "Is the National Debt a Burden?" *Oxford Economic Papers*, vol. 10 (June, 1958), p. 167.

circumstances are possible in which, for example, the criterion of fiscal neutrality dictates a budgetary deficit.)

2.1.8 The possibility of intrinsic neutrality: the veil of the fisc

We return now to the world of lump-sum taxes. In section 2.1.4 we showed that there was some level of lump-sum taxes which would neutralize an initial government debt. It was hypothesized there that $dV_0^e/d(-T_0) < 1$, meaning that an increase of the deficit (a tax reduction) could possibly induce a rise of expected future taxes but not by the amount of the increase of the deficit. Consequently, $dD_0^e/dT_0 < 0$, meaning that a tax increase (decrease) would decrease (increase) the effective government debt. Hence, in the previous analysis, there was only one tax level which would make the effective government debt equal to zero and thus neutralize an initial government debt.

But it is not inevitable that future tax expectations will conform to this hypothesis. We present in this section two cases in which tax-payers might form expectations of future taxes in such a way that *every* tax level would be neutral, which is to say that the fisc would be *intrinsically neutral* rather than neutral only at its discretion.

We show first that if the community believes the government will eventually adopt a neutral fiscal policy then $dV_0^e/d(-T_0) = 1$ must hold and moreover $D_0^e = 0$ for all T_0. We then show that the same results occur if the community believes that the government will eventually adopt a policy of continuously balanced budgets.

Suppose that the government is expected (in period 0) to adopt a neutral policy in period u. For simplicity it is assumed that all debt outstanding at time u will mature after $n - u$ periods. Hence, the tax level expected to prevail in period u satisfies the neutrality condition

$$T_u^e = S_u^e + B_u^e - V_u^e$$

where

$$B_u^e = \frac{S_u^e}{1 + r_{u+1}^e} + \frac{S_u^e}{(1 + r_{u+1}^e)(1 + r_{u+2}^e)} + \cdots$$

$$+ \frac{S_u^e + P_u^e}{(1 + r_{u+1}^e) \cdots (1 + r_n^e)}$$

and

$$V_u^e = \frac{T_{u+1}^e}{1 + r_{u+1}^e} + \frac{T_{u+2}^e}{(1 + r_{u+1}^e)(1 + r_{u+2}^e)} + \cdots$$

Noting that
$$V_{u-1}^e = \frac{V_u^e + T_u^e}{1 + r_u^e}$$

and
$$B_{u-1}^e + S_{u-1}^e - T_{u-1}^e = \frac{B_u^e + S_u^e}{1 + r_u^e}$$

we obtain
$$D_{u-1}^e = B_{u-1}^e + S_{u-1}^e - T_{u-1}^e - V_{u-1}^e$$
$$= \frac{B_u^e + S_u^e - V_u^e - T_u^e}{1 + r_u^e}$$
$$= 0 \quad \text{for all } T_{u-1}^e$$

Continuing the inductive argument, it follows that
$$D_0^e = 0 \quad \text{for all } T_0$$

Thus, if the government is expected, at some point in the future, to equate the budget surplus to the amount by which the value of the debt then exceeds the discounted value of subsequent expected taxes—so as to neutralize the debt—then the present discounted value of expected taxes subsequent to time 0 must equal the value of the postsurplus debt at time 0, whatever the algebraic surplus; i.e., the initial debt and the tax level will automatically be neutral.

The expectation of neutral policy in the future is only one circumstance leading to the neutrality of all present tax levels. The belief that the government will sometime in the future adopt a policy of regularly balanced budgets will also lead to the neutrality of all present tax levels. We prove this now.

Suppose that the budget is expected to be balanced for all $t \geq u$. Then $T_t^e = S_t^e$ for all $t \geq u$. This implies repeated refinancing of the principal P_u^e.

To shorten what would otherwise be a lengthy demonstration, assume that the government, recognizing that a balanced budget ($T = S$) implies repeated financing of a constant principal P_u^e, converts all its debt into consols paying S at $t = u$. Then
$$B_u^e = \frac{S}{1 + r_u^e} + \frac{S}{(1 + r_u^e)(1 + r_{u+1}^e)} + \cdots$$

But $T_t^e = S$ for all $t > u$. Hence
$$V_u^e = \frac{T_{u+1}^e}{1 + r_u^e} + \frac{T_{u+2}^e}{(1 + r_u^e)(1 + r_{u+1}^e)} + \cdots$$
$$= B_u^e$$

And $T_u{}^e = S_u$. Hence

$$D_u{}^e = S_u - T_u{}^e + B_u{}^e - V_u{}^e$$
$$= 0$$

By argument identical to the previous one for expected neutrality, we obtain $D_0{}^e = 0$ for all T_0.

2.2 Neutrality with Government Expenditure

Thus far our government has confined itself to redistributing wealth and to influencing the economy's rate of growth. Another important function of government is the provision of certain goods (commodities and services). We shall consider now the implications for neutral tax policy of two kinds of government expenditures: expenditures which supply goods for public consumption and expenditures which create public capital goods (i.e., public investments).

2.2.1 Formal conditions for fiscal neutrality

We should make clear at the outset that our concept of fiscal neutrality pertains to the level of net taxes or the algebraic budgetary surplus rather than to the provision of public goods. We take the amount and kinds of public services provided by the government as given. Insofar as the fisc (rather than the office of conscription) has to finance these expenditures, its only responsibility in our model is to determine what mix of taxes and borrowing (or lending) would constitute neutral financing. What is the criterion for neutral tax policy in the presence of government expenditures which have to be financed by taxes or borrowing?

In the model without government expenditure, we defined as neutral any tax policy which would produce the resource allocation which would be produced if there were no debt and no taxes (other than those offsetting taxes and transfers required to redistribute wealth in the desired way). We define neutrality analogously in the general case in which there may be government expenditures.

Suppose that the government has a program, extending over all future periods, of public services (public consumption and public investment) that it wishes to provide. Let the government "finance" this program by conscription: the government drafts resources (land, labor, and capital) in the first period to provide the public goods programmed in the first period; and it announces the future conscriptions required to provide the public goods programmed for the future. Of course, for economic efficiency, the government must conscript resources so as to minimize *social cost*, the amount of private goods that must be forgone in consequence of the diversion of resources. Meanwhile, the government will use offsetting taxes and transfers to redistribute wealth. (It is likely that the victims of conscription will receive the largest redistributive transfers.) But we suppose that net taxes and the public debt are equal to zero: the fisc is not employed to finance the program of public services.

The equilibrium which results in this situation (we call it a neutral equilibrium) is the touchstone for deciding whether or not the fisc is neutral when public services are not obtained by conscription and the fisc is used to finance these services. Suppose the inputs necessary to provide the public services are purchased by the government in the marketplace rather than drafted; then the fisc must finance these purchases by net taxes or borrowing. We shall say that tax policy is neutral if and only if the same neutral equilibrium results in this latter situation as would have resulted in the debtless conscription situation.

This may seem to be a bizarre and arbitrary basis for defining neutrality. Yet what could be a safer course of action for the government than conscription (supposing efficient conscription to be feasible) if it were intent upon leaving the allocation of resources between private consumption and private investment to the decision of the private market? Conscription would make clear what the program of public services planned would cost the community (in terms of its net worth); it would make clear by what amount the present value of their private consumption possibilities had decreased as a result of the public goods program. It is precisely the existence of a government debt and, more importantly, the practice of acquiring resources for public purposes through market purchase—which forces the fisc to decide how these purchases shall be financed, with resulting effects upon private investment—that make fiscal nonneutrality possible. In short, "no fisc" (save for the activity of wealth redistribution) is a neutral fisc.

But as we have already suggested, fiscal neutrality does not require the method of conscription any more than it requires the absence of government debt. If the resources to produce public goods are purchased through the market, neutrality can be achieved by levying the appropriate amount of lump-sum taxes.

Once again we can derive the formal conditions which must be satisfied by the fiscal variables T_0, $V_0{}^e$, etc., for fiscal neutrality. Again we shall see that if a certain sum that we shall call the *effective government debt*—which now includes the current and future obligations arising from government expenditure—is equal to zero, then tax policy is neutral.

Consider the "standard" equilibrium produced under efficient conscription with no debt and no net taxes. The first-period consumption, say $\hat{C}_0$, and hence the next-period capital stock $\hat{K}_1$ will be a function of the net worth expected in that situation, $\hat{W}_0{}^e$. Let $\hat{R}_0$ denote the equilibrium "rental value" of all land and labor in the economy (conscripted or not); that is, $\hat{R}_0$ values all land and labor at their equilibrium market rental rate and wage rate, respectively. Let $\hat{Z}_0{}^e$ denote the present discounted value of the stream of anticipated rental values $\hat{R}_1{}^e$, $\hat{R}_2{}^e$, ...

But, of course, expected net worth will be less than the sum of K_o, $\hat{R}_0$, and $\hat{Z}_0{}^e$ because of the conscriptions announced by the government. A moment's reflection reveals that if we let G_0 denote the market value of resources conscripted in the first period and let H_0 denote the present discounted value of the market's valuation of resources to be conscripted in the future, then

$$\hat{W}_0{}^e = K_o + \hat{R}_0 + \hat{Z}_0{}^e - G_0 - H_0$$

In this equation, G_0 is defined by

$$G_0 = \bar{K}_0 + \bar{R}_0$$

where $\bar{K}_0$ is the amount of capital conscripted in the first period and $\bar{R}_0$ the market (rental) value of the labor and land services conscripted in the first period. Similarly, H_0 is defined by

$$H_0 = \frac{\bar{K}_1 + \bar{R}_1}{1 + \hat{r}_1} + \frac{\bar{K}_2 + \bar{R}_2}{(1 + \hat{r}_1)(1 + \hat{r}_2{}^e)} + \cdots + \frac{\bar{K}_t + \bar{R}_t}{(1 + \hat{r}_1) \cdots (1 + \hat{r}_t{}^e)}$$

where $\bar{K}_t$ is the amount of capital to be conscripted in period t, $\bar{R}_t$ is the market value of the labor and land services to be conscripted in period t, and $\hat{r}_t^e$ is the interest rate expected to prevail in period t.

Thus far, we have been discussing the situation under conscription without debt and net taxes. If all resources employed in the production of public services are *purchased in the market* at least cost, then G_0 is just the market value of government purchases in the first period and H_0 is the present discounted value of future programmed government expenditures. These expenditures constitute income for the owners of the resources thus employed. In this case, allowing for a government debt and nonzero net taxes, expected net worth satisfies the relation

$$W_0^e = K_o + R_0 + Z_0^e + S_o + B_0 - T_0 - V_0^e$$

where the rents of course include the income to land and labor from public employment. Consumers will choose from sequences of private consumption whose present discounted value equals W_0^e as given by this relation; this choice determines the first-period consumption.

If tax policy is neutral, then $W_0^e = \hat{W}_0^e$, $R_0 = \hat{R}_0$, and $Z_0^e = \hat{Z}_0^e$, for then the same equilibrium will be produced as would be produced under conscription. Hence, if tax policy is neutral, T_0 must be such as to produce the following equality:

$$\hat{W}_0^e = K_o + \hat{R}_0 + \hat{Z}_0^e + S_o + B_0 - T_0 - V_0^e$$

But we obtained earlier that in a neutral equilibrium

$$\hat{W}_0^e = K_o + \hat{R}_0 + \hat{Z}_0^e - G_0 - H_0$$

Therefore, for neutrality, T_0 must satisfy the equation

$$S_0 + B_0 - T_0 - V_0^e = -G_0 - H_0$$

or $$G_0 + H_0 + S_o + B_0 - T_0 - V_0^e = 0$$

This result states that for fiscal neutrality, the present discounted value of present and future taxes, $T_0 + V_0^e$, should equal the present discounted value of present and future government "obligations," $G_0 + H_0 + S_o + B_0$. We shall call the excess of the latter over the former—i.e., the left-hand side of the above equation—the *effective government debt*, and we shall denote it by D_0^e. Hence the result states that for fiscal neutrality the effective government debt should be zero: $D_0^e = 0$. Otherwise expected net worth would be different from what it would be in the conscription situation, with the result that consumption and next-period capital would be different as well.

Our finding is hardly surprising. It simply means that given some program of public services, if in case the services are obtained by market purchases the fisc wishes to have the same effect upon consumption as the office of conscription would have were it assigned to acquire the resources for public use, it must tax in such a way that people feel impoverished by the same amount as they would by conscription.

2.2.2 Neutral financing of expenditures for public consumption

We shall consider now the relation between the neutral tax level and the level of government consumption expenditures. Government expenditures for public investment will be introduced in the next section. Our results on the neutralization of the government debt showed that a balanced budget need not be neutral. It might be conjectured, however, that neutrality requires financing the whole of government expenditures (as distinct from the debt service) by taxes. But this is not generally correct, as we shall now show.

Consider a small increase of first-period expenditures for public consumption, the present value of planned future government expenditures and the value of the initial debt being held constant. Let G_0^c denote the level of expenditures for present public consumption in the first period, and let H_0^c denote the present discounted value of planned future expenditures for public consumption. Under what conditions will it be neutral to finance the increase of G_0^c by an equal increase of T_0? That is, under what conditions does $D_0^e = 0$ imply $dT_0/dG_0^c = 1$?

For neutrality we require that

$$dD_0^e = dG_0^c - dT_0 - dV_0^e = 0$$

From the above equation it follows that

$$\frac{dT_0}{dG_0^c} = 1 - \frac{dV_0^e}{dG_0^c}$$

Of course G_0^c could influence V_0^e directly and through its effect upon the neutral tax level. We may write

$$\frac{dV_0^e}{dG_0^c} = \frac{\partial V_0^e}{\partial G_0^c} + \frac{\partial V_0^e}{\partial T_0}\frac{dT_0}{dG_0^c}$$

Substituting the latter equation into the former, we finally obtain

$$\frac{dT_0}{dG_0{}^c} = \frac{1 - \partial V_0{}^e / \partial G_0{}^c}{1 + \partial V_0{}^e / \partial T_0}$$

In order to evaluate $dT_0/dG_0{}^c$, we therefore need to know how future expected taxes depend upon T_0 and $G_0{}^c$; that is, we need to know $\partial V_0{}^e / \partial T_0$ and $\partial V_0{}^e / \partial G_0{}^c$. Let us adopt the following hypothesis about the determination of the present value of expected future net taxes,

$$V_0{}^e = \psi(G_0{}^c + S_0 + B_0 - T_0, T_0, H_0{}^c, G_0{}^c)$$

where $0 \leq \psi_1 < 1$, $\psi_2 \geq 0$, $0 \leq \psi_3 < 1$.

The presence of the first two terms needs no comment. The first is a *debt or deficit effect*, the second a *tax-extrapolation effect*. They were hypothesized earlier. The presence of the last two arguments of this function—arguments which did not appear when government expenditures were supposed nil—deserves comment. First, it would be preferable to suppose that $V_0{}^e$ is a function of the present discounted value of the future expenditures which the community *expects* the government to make, say $(H_0{}^c)^e$, rather than the present value of the expenditures which the government calculates will be required by the planned program of public consumption, $H_0{}^c$. However, we shall suppose these variables are equal (as they would be if the government made public its expenditure projections). The last term, $G_0{}^c$, is introduced on the ground that $V_0{}^e$ might depend upon present and future interest rates—it surely will unless expected future taxes vary with interest rates in such a way as to keep their present discounted value $V_0{}^e$ constant—and these interest rates might vary with the level of government expenditure (for they may affect private investment). Hence ψ_4 may have a nonzero value. (We shall refer to ψ_4 as the *revaluation effect* on $V_0{}^e$ of the change in interest rates accompanying the change of $G_0{}^c$.)

On this hypothesis our previous result becomes

$$\frac{dT_0}{dG_0{}^c} = \frac{1 - (\psi_1 + \psi_4)}{1 - \psi_1 + \psi_2}$$

It can be seen that if $-\psi_4 < \psi_2$ then $dT_0/dG_0{}^c < 1$, meaning that for neutrality a certain amount of debt financing of the increment in government expenditure would be neutral. But none of these inequalities is a necessary consequence of our assumptions, so that $dT_0/dG_0^c = 1$ or $dT_0/dG_0^c > 1$ is also possible.

More decisive results can be obtained if we suppose that the change of G_0^c (when neutrally financed) has only a negligible effect upon interest rates, hence only a negligible revaluation effect upon V_0^e. This is plausible if we are considering only an infinitesimal change of government expenditure. In this case

$$\frac{dT_0}{dG_0^c} = \frac{1 - \psi_1}{1 - \psi_1 + \psi_2}$$

Since $\psi_2 \geq 0$, it follows that $dT_0/dG_0^c \leq 1$. If $\psi_2 > 0$—meaning that there is a positive tax-extrapolation effect—then $dT_0/dG_0^c < 1$, meaning that for neutrality some of the expenditure should be financed by government borrowing.

This last result should be obvious. Supposing that the first-period increase of government expenditure is not to be repeated in the future, full tax financing of the "extraordinary" expenditure would reduce expected net worth by more than the cost of the public consumption (equals the value of the expenditure) if people extrapolated the present tax level into the future: it would make the effective government debt negative and reduce consumption below the level that would be produced under the conscription method. We saw earlier that a balanced budget would not generally neutralize a government debt. This last result shows again that a balanced budget is not necessarily neutral.

We have considered the neutral financing of varying present government expenditures while planned future public consumption is held constant. "Permanent" changes of the level of government expenditures for public consumption also deserve analysis.

Consider first an increase of H_0^c, holding constant the amount of first-period government expenditure G_0^c. By an analysis identical to that used above we find that for $D_0^e = 0$,

$$\frac{dT_0}{dH_0^c} = \frac{1 - \partial V_0^e/\partial H_0^c}{1 + \partial V_0^e/\partial T_0}$$

or
$$\frac{dT_0}{dH_0^c} = \frac{1 - \psi_3}{1 - \psi_1 + \psi_2}$$

Since $\psi_3 < 1$, this expression is greater than 0. This result, while obvious to any reader who has ventured this far, merits some emphasis: for neutrality a rise in planned *future* public consumption requires an increase of taxes in the *present*. Therefore, sufficiently large future planned expenditures would require that the government run a budgetary surplus. This tax policy would presumably (the matter depends somewhat upon the character of the future government expenditures) depress consumption and thus raise the economy's rate of growth.

Consider now a joint change of G_0^c and H_0^c. From the formulas for dT_0/dG_0^c and dT_0/dH_0^c obtained above we find that

$$\frac{dT_0}{dG_0^c} \gtreqless 1$$

according as $\qquad \dfrac{dH_0^c}{dG_0^c} \gtreqless \dfrac{\partial V_0^e/\partial T_0 + \partial V_0^e/\partial G_0^c}{1 - \partial V_0^e/\partial H_0^c}$

If we neglect any change of interest rates, this condition reduces to

$$\frac{dT_0}{dG_0^c} \gtreqless 1$$

according as $\qquad \dfrac{dH_0^c}{dG_0^c} \gtreqless \dfrac{\psi_2}{1 - \psi_3}$

or $\qquad \psi_2 + \dfrac{dH_0^c}{dG_0^c} \psi_3 \lesseqgtr \dfrac{dH_0^c}{dG_0^c}$

(The left-hand side of the last inequality is just dV_0^e/dG_0^c when $dT_0/dG_0^c = 1$ and interest rates are fixed.) Clearly everything depends upon the magnitude of dH_0^c/dG_0^c.

As a special case suppose that the change of government expenditure planned in period t, G_t^c, is equal to the change of expenditure in the first period. Then

$$\frac{dG_1^c}{dG_0^c} = \frac{dG_2^c}{dG_0^c} = \cdots = 1$$

and $\qquad \dfrac{dH_0^c}{dG_0^c} = \dfrac{1}{1 + r_1} + \dfrac{1}{(1 + r_1)(1 + r_2^e)} + \cdots$

It is clear that the values of ψ_2 and ψ_3 need not satisfy the equality $\psi_2 + (dH_0^c/dG_0^c)\psi_3 = dH_0^c/dG_0^c$, so that $dT_0/dG_0^c = 1$ need not be neutral.

But full tax financing of the increase of government expenditure *will* be neutral on a variety of special hypotheses about V_0^e. For example, suppose that $\psi_3 = 0$ and that $dT_1^e/dT_0 = dT_2^e/dT_0 = \cdots = 1$. Then

$$\frac{dV_0^e}{dT_0} = \frac{1}{1+r_1} + \frac{1}{(1+r_1)(1+r_2^e)} + \cdots$$

Since $dV_0^e/dT_0 = \psi_2$ when $dT_0/dG_0^c = 1$ and $\psi_3 = 0$, we have in this case $\psi_2 = dH_0^c/dG_0^c$ and therefore $dT_0/dG_0^c = 1$ for neutrality.

Of course, this is budget balancing only "at the margin." The initial values of B_0, H_0^c, and G_0^c may call for an unbalanced budget. But on certain special hypotheses and conditions a totally balanced budget would be neutral.

Suppose that $B_0 = S_0 = 0$, that $G_0^c = G_1^c = \cdots = G_t^c = \cdots$, and that $T_0 = T_1^e = \cdots = T_t^e = \cdots$. Then

$$D_0^e = G_0^c + H_0^c - T_0 - V_0^e$$
$$= G_0^c \left[1 + \frac{1}{1+r_1} + \frac{1}{(1+r_1)(1+r_2^e)} + \cdots \right]$$
$$- T_0 \left[1 + \frac{1}{1+r_1} + \frac{1}{(1+r_1)(1+r_2^e)} + \cdots \right] = 0$$

if $\qquad\qquad G_0^c = T_0$

Many writers who have asserted the neutrality of balanced budgets may have had in mind an economy which satisfies these conditions. As we have just shown, a balanced budget would indeed be neutral in such an economy.

But while stationary expenditure plans and stationary tax expectations are appropriate to a stationary state, they are unlikely to be found in growing economies. Consider the following special situation, one which might arise in a growing economy. There is a constant relative rate of increase of planned government expenditures and a smaller constant rate of increase of expected taxes.

$$\frac{G_{t+1}^c - G_t^c}{G_t^c} = \gamma > 0 \qquad \text{for all } t \geq 0$$

$$\frac{T_1^e - T_0}{T_0} = \frac{T_{t+1}^e - T_t^e}{T_t^e} = \tau < \gamma \qquad \text{for all } t \geq 1$$

Then clearly $G_0^c + H_0^c - T_0 - V_0^e = 0$ if and only if $T_0 > G_0^c$. If tax financing of the debt service neutralizes or less than neutralizes the debt, then $D_0{}^e = S_o + B_0 + G_0{}^c + H_0{}^c - T_0 - V_0{}^e = 0$ if and only if $T_0 > S_o + G_0{}^c$.

One conclusion to be drawn from this section is that neutrality requires deficits in some circumstances, surpluses in others, and budget balance only exceptionally. Our last finding seems especially interesting: in an economy in which government plans call for a trend in expenditures for public consumption which rises substantially faster than the tax-payment trend expected by the community, neutrality requires a budgetary surplus.[1]

2.2.3 Neutral financing of expenditures for public investment

In this section, we shall investigate the neutral financing of government capital expenditures. For those readers who do not wish to pursue this analysis, we shall anticipate our conclusions. A neutral fisc will not find it useful to distinguish between the total government debt and the *deadweight debt*—the excess of the debt over the value of the public capital stock. Second, a neutral fisc will not establish a capital budget—a separate budget for all capital expenditures—which is routinely financed by borrowing; there is no presumption that for neutrality, public investments should be financed by borrowing to a greater degree than public consumptions. These conclusions refer to government-owned capital goods of the kind which produce "public goods" in Samuelson's sense—i.e., goods for which no price to users should be charged if Pareto optimality is to be attained. Different conclusions apply to government investments which are like private investments in that the investment outlay is recouped by charges to the users of the goods produced by the capital. Where the government acts like a business, it is neutral for it to finance its capital outlays like a business, by issuing securities; but only there.

To demonstrate the first of our conclusions, we consider the implications for neutral taxation of the existence of a fixed stock of public

---

[1] An important footnote to this discussion is the following: "Neutrality" (meaning $dV_0{}^e/dT_0 = -1$) no longer implies *fiscal neutrality* in our sense of the term when future government expenditures are planned. For if $V_0{}^e = S_o + B_0 + G_0 - T_0$ for all T_0 ("neutrality"), then $D_0{}^e = H_0 > 0$ for all T_0 (fiscal nonneutrality). However, there is also "neutrality" if $V_0{}^e = S_o + B_0 + G_0 + H_0 - T_0$ for all T_0; in this case "neutrality" does guarantee fiscal neutrality toward growth.

capital. If this public capital (a lighthouse, for example) aids in the
production of the private good, we may take this into account by
writing the production function

$$K_{t+1} = F(K_t - C_t, L_t, N_t; K_G)$$

where K_G denotes the quantity of public capital. If the public capital
(a missile installation, for example) aids in the production of some
public good, we may take it into account similarly in the production
function of the public good.

Thus the initial quantity of public capital figures in the production
function as a parameter, like the fertility of the soil or any other fixed
factor affecting the productivity of land, labor, and capital (the private
good). Since the foregoing analysis of neutral taxation holds for any
production function having the properties specified, the presence of
public capital in the economy requires no amendment of that analysis:
it is valid for any quantity of public capital, just as for land of any
fertility.

It is sometimes suggested that only deadweight debt (government
debt not "backed" by an equal value of government capital) is a
"burden," and accordingly it might be thought that for fiscal neutrality, only the deadweight debt needs to be neutralized. But the above
observation shows that it makes no difference for the neutral tax level
whether, for example, the rain which makes crops grow is produced by
a government rainmaking machine or falls from natural causes: the
difference is only in the interpretation of the parameter.

The notion that an unneutralized debt is required to represent the
stock of public capital rests possibly on the assumption that the community will neglect the stream of income generated by the public capital and hence needs to hold an equal (unneutralized) debt if it is to
believe itself to be as wealthy as it truly is. This is, of course, an
optimality argument, not a neutrality argument; a neutral policy seeks
only to make people believe they are as wealthy as they would believe
they were under the conscription-and-no-debt system. To the extent
that people misestimate their wealth, and so their consumption possibilities—say, because they underestimate the contribution to their
consumption possibilities made by public capital goods—a neutral
policy may not be optimal. Of course, optimality is our ultimate objec-

tive. But we know of no reason to believe that consumers underestimate that portion of their future income attributable to public capital to any greater degree than they may underestimate that portion of their future incomes attributable to natural endowments (like the fertility of the soil). At any rate, it is clear that if the community correctly estimates its future income, its present discounted value will already include the capitalized value of the "returns" attributable to public capital; in that case, there is no rationale for letting government debt backed by public capital go unneutralized.

Consider now the neutral financing of a small increase of government expenditures, dG_0^k, for increasing the stock of public capital. Suppose that expenditures for current public consumption, the present value of all future government expenditures, and the value of the initial debt are held constant.

The formal conditions for fiscal neutrality derived above imply that there must be an accompanying change of the tax level, dT_0, which satisfies the equation

$$0 = dG_0^k - dT_0 - dV_0^e$$

From this equation we derive

$$\frac{dT_0}{dG_0^k} = \frac{1 - \partial V_0^e/\partial G_0^k}{1 - \partial V_0^e/\partial T_0}$$

From this result it is clear there is no presumption that, for neutrality, public investments should be debt-financed, that $dT_0/dG_0^k = 0$.

Nor is there any presumption that expenditures for public investment require, for neutrality, proportionately less tax finance (hence proportionately greater debt finance) than do expenditures for public consumption. Consider a small increase of the former, coupled with an equal decrease of the latter: $dG_0^c = -dG_0^k$. Then for neutrality,

$$0 = -dT_0 - dV_0^e$$

if we hold constant the present value of all future government expenditures and the value of the initial government debt. Hence

$$\left(\frac{dT_0}{dG_0^k}\right)_{G_0^k + G_0^c = \text{const}} = \frac{\partial V_0^e/\partial G_0^c - \partial V_0^e/\partial G_0^k}{1 + \partial V_0^e/\partial T_0}$$

It is the difference $\partial V_0^e/\partial G_0^c - \partial V_0^e/\partial G_0^k$ which determines the sign of

$dT_0/dG_0{}^k$. Clearly, if public investments promote the expectation of future taxes more than public consumption, meaning $\partial V_0{}^e/\partial G_0{}^c < \partial V^e/\partial G_0{}^k$, then $dT_0/dG_0{}^k < 0$; taxes would have to be reduced. But whether this is so seems problematical.

The notion—which we have shown to be inconsistent with neutrality —that public investments should be debt-financed may originate in the fact that many firms issue debt to finance much of their capital expenditures. But the typical private investment bears only a weak analogy to the kind of public investment considered here in that we supposed that no charge was made to private users for the services of the public capital goods. There ought to be no charge to users of government capital which produces "public goods" in the sense of Samuelson; the services of such capital can be shared by users and therefore do not need to be rationed by a price to users. But a user charge would be indicated for the services of other kinds of government capital. This is the capital in what might be called the "socialized" sector of the economy.

Let us then consider neutral taxation when there are government investments in capital goods for the services of which it is appropriate to charge users. Denote by X_0 the rents earned by government capital in the first period and by Y_0 the present discounted value of the rents which the government expects to earn from the sale of services of the government capital it plans to provide in the future. In this situation, with revenues accruing to the socialized sector, the government will recognize that even a policy of conscription and the absence of debt would not make consumers sovereign over aggregate saving and investment. To be neutral, the government must, in addition to conscripting, make net transfer payments in an amount such that the present discounted value of the present and expected future transfers just equals the present discounted value of the present and expected future rents accruing to the government from the socialized sector, $X_0 + Y_0$. If this is done, the economy will behave as if the capital of the socialized sector were privately owned.[1] Under a neutral policy, therefore, the present discounted value of the sequence of planned consumption

[1] The proposition that a socialist state must, for consumer sovereignty over investment, pay out a social dividend equal to the revenues of the socialized sector, a proposition that is in the spirit of the above proposition in the text, has been argued by F. J. Atkinson, "Saving and Investment in a Socialist State," *Review of Economic Studies*, vol. 15, no. 2, (1947–1948), pp. 78–83.

(including now the consumption of the services of the socialized sector) is given by

$$\hat{W}_0^e = K_o + \hat{R}_0 + X_0 + \hat{Z}_0^e + Y_0 - G_0 - H_0$$

Without conscription, with the government taxing to finance government expenditures and making no transfers of the rents from the socialized sector, expected net worth is given by

$$W_0^e = K_o + R_0 + Z_0^e + S_o + B_0 - T_0 - V_0^e$$

If tax policy is to be neutral, it must make $W_0^e = \hat{W}_0^e$, $R_0 = \hat{R}_0$, and $Z_0^e = \hat{Z}_0^e$. Hence for neutrality, T_0 must satisfy

$$\hat{W}_0^e = K_o + \hat{R}_0 + \hat{Z}_0^e + S_o + B_0 - T_0 - V_0^e$$

Therefore, the neutral tax level must satisfy the equation

$$K_o + \hat{R}_0 + \hat{Z}_0^e + S_o + B_0 - T_0 - V_0^e$$
$$= K_0 + \hat{R}_0 + \hat{X}_0 + \hat{Z}_0^e + \hat{Y}_0 - \hat{G}_0 - \hat{H}_0$$

or $\quad G_0 + H_0 + S_o + B_0 - X_0 - Y_0 - T_0 - V_0^e = 0$

The result states that for neutrality the present value of present and future expected taxes should be reduced by the amount of the present value of the rentals expected on government capital for fixed G_0, H_0, S_o, and B_0. The reduction of the taxes is a way of transferring the rents to the consumer.

What are the implications of this result for the neutral financing of government investments for which there are user charges? An example of considerable interest is the following: Suppose that there is a small investment in government capital which costs dG_0^k and which is expected to bring in additional user charges whose present discounted value $dX_0 + dY_0$ is equal to the cost dG_0^k. Suppose that all other government expenditures, present and future, as well as the value of the initial debt are fixed. Then for neutrality, the change in the net tax level, dT_0, must satisfy the equality

$$dG_0^k - dX_0 - dY_0 - dT_0 - dV_0^e = 0$$

whence $\quad \dfrac{dT_0}{dG_0^k} = \dfrac{-\partial V_0^e/\partial G_0^k}{1 + \partial V_0^e/\partial T_0}$

since $\quad 1 - \dfrac{dX_0}{dG_0^k} - \dfrac{dY_0}{dG_0^k} = 0$

If we suppose that any debt issued to finance the government investment is labeled a special issue to be financed out of anticipated user charges, the expenditure dG_0^k will have no direct effect upon V_0^e except as the investment alters present and expected future interest rates and hence the present valuation of expected future taxes. Therefore, if there is only a negligible change of present and expected future interest rates, $\partial V^e/\partial G_0^k$ will be equal to 0. In that case, $dT_0/dG_0^k = 0$, meaning that the government investment must be entirely debt-financed if the government is to be fiscally neutral.

We conclude that deficit financing of government investments whose costs are expected to be completely recovered in future user charges is approximately neutral. But deficit financing of other government investments, like the deficit financing of expenditures for public consumption, is not generally neutral.

Chapter 3

Fiscal neutrality toward growth in a monetary economy

We have now to investigate the conditions for fiscal neutrality in a monetary economy. We derive the expression for the neutral level of taxation as a function of the government-owned central bank's demand liabilities—which would constitute the money supply if there were no private banks—and the capitalized value of the (algebraic) net earnings of the central bank. We conclude the chapter with some remarks about the functions of the central bank, which are to control aggregate demand and to provide the economy with an optimal supply of liquidity.

3.1 The Condition for Neutrality in the Presence of a Government-owned Central Bank

One could interpret the analysis of the previous chapter as applying to a monetary economy having only private banks as well as to a barter

economy. But a laissez-faire monetary system has two important
defects. First, money is not "safe" in that the value of claims against
one bank is likely to fluctuate relative to the value of claims against
other banks. The changes of supply and demand which produce such
changes in relative value are likely to be unforeseen by the holders of
the bank's money when they acquired it; as a result, the holding of such
money becomes quite risky. Hence, government controls over private
banks are necessary if money is to be "safe."

Second, a laissez-faire monetary system produces unpredictable
changes in the purchasing power of "money" in the aggregate. Periods
of unemployment may occur unless the fiscal authorities abandon, at
least temporarily, their policy of neutrality or their growth objectives.
Hence, the government requires *monetary* controls over aggregate
demand if it wishes to use government expenditures only to supply the
community with desired public goods and to use aggregate tax policy
("fiscal policy" as we have been using that term) in order to achieve the
desired growth path. From our point of view, the principal rationale of
central-bank controls over the money supply is that they permit the
regulation of aggregate demand while freeing the fiscal tool for service
of the government's growth policy (e.g., a policy of fiscal neutrality
toward growth). The consequence for the feasibility of neutral fiscal
policy of the fact that monetary policy has a delayed effect upon investment demand is discussed in section 4.10.

It would be possible, of course, for the government to charter a
private bank to act as the central bank in the monetary system. There
could be no economic objections to this so long as the private central
bank operated in the public interest. In this case, neutrality by the
fisc would simply call for neutralization of any algebraic subsidy to
the private bank which was necessary to give the bank a normal rate
of return on its capital. But what if the bank were "socialized?"

If the central bank *were* privately owned and the government had no
debt and levied no taxes but only conscripted to provide for government
expenditures, then the government would be neutral and private
wealth would be given by

$$\hat{W}_0{}^e = E_0{}^p + \hat{R}_0 + \hat{Z}_0{}^e + X_0 + Y_0 - G_0 - H_0$$

where $E_0{}^p$ is the value of the capital claims held by the nonbank public,

$\hat{R}_0$ is the wages and land rents paid by the private economy, $\hat{Z}_0^e$ is the present value of expected future wages and rents, X_0 is the value of the after-subsidy current earnings of the central bank from its service charges and holdings of capital claims, Y_0 is the present value of expected future bank earnings, G_0 is the opportunity cost of the resources conscripted by the government (including resources used to subsidize the bank), and H_0 is the present value of the resources to be conscripted in the future. Note that the money supply created by the central bank would not add to private wealth because such money would be a liability of the (private) owners of the central bank. All variables here and elsewhere (except M_o below) are in real terms.

If the government were to "socialize" the bank and if there were a fisc which levied taxes and had an initial debt, wealth would be given by

$$W_0^e = E_0^p + R_0 + Z_0^e + \frac{M_o}{p} + S_o^p + B_0^p - T_0 - V_0^e$$

where S_o^p is the interest on that part of the initial public debt in private (hence nonbank) hands, B_0^p is that part of the initial debt (valued after interest is paid) held by the nonbank public, T_0 is the level of taxes, and V_0^e is the present value of expected future taxes. M_o/p is the real value of the central bank's initial demand liabilities; this is part of the government's debt and adds to expected private wealth since it is an obligation of the government rather than private individuals.

Now, as we explained in the previous chapter, a government seeking to be neutral toward growth will choose T_0 so as to achieve the same growth path as would be achieved were the socialized sector privately owned (and operated in the public interest) and were public goods and subsidies afforded by conscription. But if T_0 is so chosen, then $W_0^e = \hat{W}_0^e$, $R_0 = \hat{R}_0$, and $Z_0^e = \hat{Z}_0^e$. And these equalities imply, from the two equations above, that

$$G_0 + H_0 + \frac{M_o}{p} + S_o^p + B_0^p - X_0 - Y_0 - T_0 - V_0^e = 0$$

The result states that for neutrality, taxes should neutralize the government's planned government expenditures, $G_0 + H_0$, plus the total government debt, $M_o/p + S_o^p + B_0^p$, *net* of the capitalized value of the earnings of the socialized enterprises, $X_0 + Y_0$. If the central bank had no earnings other than those from its holdings of private capital claims, then the latter deduction would simply constitute a netting out of the private sector's indebtedness to the government from the government's gross indebtedness to the private sector, since $X_0 + Y_0$ would represent just the value of the central bank's holdings of private securities.

It should be emphasized that the notation M_o/p denotes the real value of the central bank's demand liabilities rather than the real value of the whole money supply. Only if there were no private banks or there were a 100 per cent reserve banking system would the central bank's demand liabilities be equal to the money supply.

3.1.1 Open-market operations in a neutral fiscal regime

Neutralization of the fiscal effects of the government's ownership of the central bank has some interesting consequences for the effects of open-market operations by the central bank.

A theory of how open-market operations affect the price level, the real value of the money supply, wealth, investment, and the rate of interest was developed by Lloyd Metzler.[1] For simplicity we shall suppose, with Metzler, that the central bank is the only bank in the economy and that there is no government interest-bearing debt.

With slight modification to accord with the theory of consumption demand employed here, we can state Metzler's model in the form of the following two equations:

$$\frac{M}{p} = L(r) \qquad L'(r) < 0$$

$$C\left(r, E^p + R + Z + \frac{M}{p} - T - V\right) + I(r) = \text{const} \qquad C_r > I'(r) < 0$$

The first of these equations states that the supply of real cash balances must equal the demand, which is a function of the rate of interest. (Equilibrium income is assumed always to equal the full-employment level so that income does not appear in the demand function.) The second equation states that, in equilibrium, consumption plus investment add up to full-employment national output. The two unknowns

---

[1] Lloyd A. Metzler, "Wealth, Saving and the Rate of Interest," *Journal of Political Economy*, vol. 59 (April, 1951), pp. 93–116.

of the equations are the price level p and the rate of interest r. R and Z we shall take to be constant.

We shall use this model to analyze an open-market purchase of private securities. This action has two impacts: it reduces E^p, the stock of private securities in private hands, and it increases M, the quantity of money. We hold T and V constant.

Consider first the latter impact, holding constant the public's holdings of securities. Such a *ceteris paribus* increase of M can have no effect upon the real value of money holdings, hence the rate of interest and the "mix" between consumption and investment—only an effect upon the equilibrium price level which must change in the same proportion as M. (This assumes that the price change leaves unchanged the expected rate of price change, hence the real rate of interest.) This invariance of equilibrium "real" variables to the nominal money supply is due to the property of the two equations that M appears only as a ratio to p.

It follows that any effect of an open-market purchase upon the "real" variables such as the equilibrium rate of interest and the equilibrium level of investment must depend upon the impact of the open-market purchase upon private holdings of securities. As Metzler explained, an open-market purchase has the same effect on these real variables as a capital levy payable only in shares. As a consequence, the open-market purchase has "fiscal" effects: the reduction of E^p reduces total wealth (given M), hence reduces consumption demand. The price level will therefore fall, thus increasing the real value of money holdings and hence reducing the rate of interest by virtue of the demand-for-money equation. The fall of the interest rate induces a rise of the amount of investment just sufficient to offset the fall of consumption demand.[1]

Hence, as Metzler argued, an injection of money by means of an open-market purchase is not "neutral" in that it changes the equilibrium values of the rate of interest, the real value of the money supply, consumption, and investment. However, our analysis has assumed that T and V were held constant in the face of the fall of real total wealth. If the fisc follows a neutral policy, it will reduce taxes so as to maintain

---

[1] It can be shown that the increase of real money holdings is insufficient to offset the reduction of privately held securities, so that total real wealth falls.

total wealth at its neutral level. This action will prevent any fall of consumption demand due to the open-market purchase. Hence, equilibrium investment and the interest rate will be unchanged. By reducing $T + V$ by the amount of the central bank's acquisition of private securities, the fisc will leave the open-market purchase with only one impact, that upon the money supply. Therefore, the result of an open-market purchase, if its fiscal effects are neutralized by a tax reduction, is simply to increase the equilibrium price level in proportion to the increase of the money supply. Real wealth, the rate of interest, consumption, and investment will be the same in the new equilibrium as in the old equilibrium. Thus open-market operations are "neutral," in the classical sense, in a neutral fiscal regime.

Of course, this "neutrality" of open-market operations in no way impairs the effectiveness with which the central bank can carry out its function of controlling aggregate demand. Open-market operations remain perfectly able to control the equilibrium price level through their effect upon the money supply. Further, if prices and wage rates are "sticky" (slow to adjust to changes of their equilibrium values) so that underemployment and overemployment are possible, then this control of aggregate demand will give it power over the level of employment (though not the equilibrium level of employment which, in Metzler's neoclassical model, is always equal to "full employment").

3.2 Optimizing Liquidity

The foregoing analysis, while it shows that the effectiveness of open-market operations is unimpaired by countervailing fiscal actions designed to keep unchanged the equilibrium values of real wealth, consumption, investment, and the rate of interest, does bring out a dilemma for fiscal and monetary policy. If the rate of interest is implicitly determined by the fiscal authorities' growth policy—be that a neutral policy or the desire for some consumption-investment mix corresponding to which is some real rate of interest—then so is the *real* value of the money supply according to the demand-for-money equation. Yet an objective of the fiscal and monetary authorities should be to provide the economy with an optimal amount of liquidity—with an optimal real quantity of money. There seems to be a conflict between growth objectives and liquidity objectives. Only accidentally will there be an interest rate which yields the optimal level of liquidity, through the first equation, and at the same time yields the desired rate of investment, through the second equation.

A detailed analysis of optimal liquidity is beyond the scope of the present volume. A fuller analysis than the one to be offered here can be found in the author's paper on the welfare consequences of anticipated inflation.[1]

We may say that liquidity is optimal when the "price" effectively "charged" to holders of money is equal to the marginal social cost of supplying liquidity. But price in excess of marginal social cost need not be nonoptimal if the demand curve is perfectly price inelastic in the neighborhood of the optimum; and this is the case here, as the subsequent discussion implies. The "price" of being liquid, as Keynes wrote, is (ordinarily) the nominal rate of interest, for this is the earnings rate that must be forgone by anyone electing to hold interest-less money rather than interest-bearing assets. The marginal social cost of supplying liquidity is a more intricate matter relating to the costs incurred by the bank in sustaining an increased number of deposits (or depositors) and notes. Suffice it to say that when everyone in the economy has been brought into the monetary sector (from the barter sector) these marginal costs are zero or close to zero.

If we take the marginal cost of supplying money to be zero in the relevant range, then liquidity will be optimal only if the price of being liquid is sufficiently small so that no one is motivated, at some inconvenience, to economize on money by holding a portion of his transactions balances over a part of his income or payments period in the form of interest-bearing assets, in order to earn additional interest. When all transactions balances are held in cash, we shall say that there is *full liquidity*. We may take it for granted that liquidity is optimal only when the price of being liquid is small enough to produce full liquidity.

Thus optimal liquidity would appear to call for a very low rate of interest, probably lower than the real rate of interest corresponding to the rate of investment produced by the government's growth policy. To put the matter more formally, if r^* denotes the growth-dictated

[1] Edmund S. Phelps, "Anticipated Inflation and Economic Welfare," *Journal of Political Economy*, vol. 73, no. 1 (February, 1965), pp. 1–13.

rate of interest then, unless r^* happens to be very small, $L(r^*)$ will fall short of $(M/p)^*$, the value of real balances corresponding to full liquidity; to bring about $L(r) = (M/p)^*$ would require a value of r smaller then r^*. Fortunately, however, there is no real dilemma if the government can engineer an anticipated deflation or, alternatively, if it can pay interest on money.

The deflationary route is based on the fact that the r of the first equation is the *nominal* rate of interest, while the r of the second equation is the real rate of interest—i.e., the nominal interest rates less the expected rate of inflation. The two are equal only if the price level is expected to be stationary. By creating the expectation of a falling price trend the government could reduce the nominal rate of interest corresponding to any given real rate of interest. If r denotes the real rate of interest and ρ the expected rate of algebraic inflation, then the nominal interest rate is just $r + \rho$, and real balances in equilibrium must satisfy $M/p = L(r + \rho)$. By making ρ negative the government can make $r + \rho$ small without reducing the level of r. The fall of the nominal interest rate will increase the demand for money, producing a fall of the price level and an increase of the real value of money holdings. Thus the reduction of the nominal interest rate by means of creating the expectation of deflation would enable full liquidity to be achieved without an unwanted reduction of the real rate of interest corresponding to an unwanted alteration of the consumption-investment mix.

But to create the expectation of deflation the government would need to promote deflation. If prices and wage rates are sticky, this would produce unemployment. The deflationary route is not a practical way out of the dilemma.

The other route entails the payment of interest to holders of money. Assume that the expected rate of price change is zero. Then the "price" of being liquid, of which the demand for money is a function, is no longer the (nominal and real) interest rate r but rather $r - \mu$, where μ is the own rate of interest on money. By paying interest on money the central bank can reduce the price of being liquid sufficiently to produce full liquidity. To put the matter more formally, the parameter μ constitutes a third policy weapon which, together with M and T, permits the central bank and the fisc to control three variables: p, r, and M/p. (We take E to be a function of M and T so that M, T, and μ are the only independently controllable policy parameters.) With only M and T in its control, the government can choose only those combinations $(r, M/p)$ which are consistent with the equation $M/p = L(r)$. But by introducing the parameter μ, the government can shift the locus of feasible $(r, M/p)$ so that it now satisfies the equation $M/p = L(r - \mu)$; by appropriate choice of μ this locus can be made to pass through the desired point, say $[r^*, (M/p)^*]$. For a detailed analysis the reader is again referred to the author's paper on anticipated inflation.[1]

We have shown that both the government's growth policy and optimal liquidity can be achieved, even with a stationary rather than a falling expected price trend, if the government will pay interest on money. It is a short step to the conclusion that both growth and liquidity objectives can be met even if the expected price trend is rising. A standard objection to inflation, even fully anticipated inflation, is that it increases the price of liquidity, for it raises the nominal rate of interest associated with any real rate of interest; this "price" rise manifests itself in costly efforts to economize on money and a resulting fall in the real value of money holdings. Liquidity falls short of the optimum by an even greater amount than when prices are expected to be stationary.[2] But if a suitable interest rate on money is paid, this will not happen. The central bank can increase μ by the amount of the expected rate of inflation and thus maintain the price of being liquid at its optimal level.

If the expected trend of prices need make no difference for liquidity—because the central bank can offset its liquidity effect by suitable adjustment of the own rate of interest on money—then the question arises: What is the optimal trend of prices? While achievement of a liquidity optimum is not one of them (if interest can be paid on money), there are efficiency grounds for choosing between alternative price trends. Two of them have something to do with the need to denominate money and prices in discrete units.

First, a nonstationary general price trend may require sellers to change their price lists more frequently than would be required if the

[1] *Ibid.*

[2] See, for example, Martin J. Bailey, "The Welfare Cost of Inflationary Finance," *Journal of Political Economy*, vol. 64 (April, 1956), pp. 93–110. Bailey and others have held the real rate of interest fixed. For a more general analysis see the author's paper, *op. cit.*

general level of prices were fairly stationary. Second, a nonzero trend of prices will necessitate a series of currency reforms in order to maintain supplies of coins and notes in optimal denominations. Clearly, if the price level should double, the smallest coin which was optimal before should be replaced by one whose denomination is twice as great.

If it were agreed that whateverprice-trend policy were chosen it should be one that the government announces and guarantees and hence that everyone anticipates, these two might be the only desiderata. But it has been argued that the government should continuously raise the price level faster than the public anticipates in order to stimulate employment. If factor and goods markets were perfectly competitive, there would be no justification for such a policy: it would create involuntary overfull employment. But when factor markets are imperfect, the benefits may, at least for a period, outweigh the costs.

The question of optimal price policy deserves substantial analysis which we cannot provide here. Our conclusion is simply that the government can pursue whatever price policy is best and at the same time meet its growth and liquidity objectives.

Chapter 4

A critique
of neutralism

The preceding chapters have explained what we mean by a neutral policy toward economic growth. A neutral fiscal-monetary policy causes the allocation of resources to duplicate the resource allocation that would occur if the given program of government-supplied goods and services were "financed" by the efficient conscription of resources to produce them. We found that a neutral fiscal-monetary policy would reduce "expected wealth" (below what it would be without taxes and debt) by the amount of the present discounted value of the costs of the program of government expenditures plus the value of the initial public debt. A neutral policy seeks to "impoverish" people by the amount of the costs (appropriately discounted) of the (free) services which the government plans to provide.

The question before us now is: Under what conditions would a neutral policy produce a growth path of private consumer goods which is Pareto-optimal from the standpoint of the present generation? Or, equivalently, under what conditions would efficient conscription of resources produce a Pareto-optimal allocation?

4.1 Conditions for Pareto Optimality of Fiscal Neutrality

Let us consider an economy in which everyone in the population knows he will live for a certain number of years. To begin with, we suppose that there are no heirs, or more precisely no successors for whom the present population "cares." We take as given the quantities of public goods which the government plans to supply over each year of the population's life.

The growth path of "private" (nonpublic) consumption goods is said to be Pareto-optimal if there is no reallocation of resources (government expenditures being taken as given) which, by affecting the growth path of private consumption goods, will make any individual better off (over his lifetime) without making one or more other individuals worse off.

What are the conditions for such a Pareto optimum? Assuming for simplicity that all goods are produced and consumed in positive amounts, the necessary conditions are (1) that the consumption path be "efficient," i.e., that it be undominated by any other consumption path and (2) that the path equate the marginal social rate of substitution between any two goods (e.g., the consumption of a commodity at one date and the consumption of that same commodity at another date), for every individual, to the marginal social rate of transformation between those two goods.

Suppose now that the government were to conscript the resources needed to supply the programmed government services, announcing the conscription which will be necessary to supply government services in the future. Under what conditions will the private market then produce a Pareto-optimal growth path of "private" consumption goods? Sufficient conditions are:

1.   A competitive equilibrium exists and is attained.
2.   There is perfect information about current and future prices (including interest rates and wage rates) over the lifetime of the

population and also perfect information about current and future supplies of public goods.

3. Producers have perfect information about current and future technology over the lifetime of the population.

4. There are no externalities in production.

5. Consumers have perfect information about current and future tastes over their lifetime, and these preferences are unchanging over time.

6. There are no externalities in consumption other than the public goods whose production we take as given.

The first four conditions guarantee that marginal private rates of transformation equal marginal social rates of transformation and that these rates of transformation are measured by market rates of interest between one date and another date. Conditions *1*, *2*, *5*, and *6* guarantee that marginal private rates of substitution equal marginal social rates of substitution and that these rates of substitution are measured by market rates of interest. These conditions together guarantee that marginal private (hence social) rates of substitution will be equated to marginal private (hence social) rates of transformation. Hence these are the conditions for a Pareto-optimal growth path of private consumption goods.[1]

Now, if these are the conditions under which efficient conscription would permit competitive markets to achieve a Pareto-optimal growth path of "private" consumption goods, then they are also the conditions under which a neutral fiscal-monetary policy would permit Pareto optimality. For a neutral policy (by definition) duplicates the allocation of resources produced by efficient conscription.

A point of considerable interest concerns condition 2 on the knowledge of current and future prices. The only way in which this condition could be met in practice is through the use of futures markets. And the comprehensive use of futures markets would be possible only if the government adopted a neutral policy (or used conscription). For if

[1] Of course, if the government's conscriptions are to be efficient, it must also have perfect information about current and future prices and about current and future technology relating to the production of public goods.

people are to know their future disposable income, hence disposable wealth, on the basis of which they can contract to purchase goods for future delivery, they must know their future tax liabilities. These tax payments will have to be contracted for in advance, in the first period. What must these future tax liabilities be equal to? Assuming for simplicity that there is no initial public debt, they must be equal in present discounted value to the present discounted value of the government's program of public expenditures, since on balance, over their lifetime, the population will neither lend to nor borrow from the government (i.e., the population will die being neither a creditor of nor a debtor to the government). Hence, with comprehensive futures markets, the population will plan on current plus future taxes equal in present value to the present value of the factor costs of the government's programmed public expenditures; government policy is necessarily neutral in such an economy.

In such a perfect "futures economy" the function of prices (including discounted future prices, or "present prices" as they are sometimes called) is to inform consumers of the costs in terms of other goods that must be forgone of consuming more of any good (at any date). The function of taxes is to inform consumers of the cost in terms of private goods of the government's program of supplying public goods. The desirability of this function lies not so much in helping consumers to decide (through the polls) how much in the way of public goods they wish to be supplied as in helping consumers to achieve an optimal private consumption plan. The function served by a neutral policy in this perfect futures economy is to cause consumers, when they are making their consumption-saving decisions, to feel as rich as they really are (in terms of what they can feasibly consume over their lifetime).

The above propositions are not affected if we suppose that the present population will be replaced when it dies by a new generation of producers and consumers. We may suppose also that some or all members of the present population have "heirs" to whom they wish to make bequests. (But we suppose that there is only one "benefactor" for each "heir.") In this case the capital which a member of the present generation leaves to his heir could be considered an additional good that belongs in his utility function. Alternatively, the lifetime wealth the heir is expected to have might go into the utility function. The consumption plans of the present population now include these bequests.

If conditions 1 to 6 hold and if the government follows a neutral policy, then a Pareto optimum from the standpoint of the present generation will be achieved. But the presence of heirs requires reinterpretation of some of these conditions. Condition 6, that there are no externalities in consumption, now must be taken to mean that neither the consumption of one's contemporaries nor the consumption of members of the future generation (other than one's heirs) enters into the utility function of any member of the present generation.[1]

Second, with respect to condition 2, if it is not the bequest as such that has utility but rather the welfare of one's heirs—as measured, say, by their wealth—then not only must the prices and government expenditures over the lifetime of the present generation be known but also the prices and government expenditures prevailing over the lifetime of the next generation; in short, each member of the present population must know the private consumption possibilities and public goods consumption of his heir. However, if it is only the bequest as such that has utility, independently of the welfare of the heir, then this reinterpretation of condition 2 is not required.

In the model being considered, in which members of the present generation have heirs among the succeeding generation, it would be possible for the government to be a net borrower from the present generation; the present generation could bequeath any holdings of government debt to its heirs so that members of the present generation might be willing to buy government debt even though expecting to die while holding that debt. But such a government policy would not be neutral. A neutral policy will neutralize the effect upon wealth and hence consumption (and bequests) of any public debt held at the beginning of each period by levying a suitable amount of taxes. In the

---

[1] If some members of the present generation shared a concern for the welfare of one or more members of the next generation—in other words, some heirs had more than one benefactor—then the Baumol-Sen-Marglin *isolation paradox* would come into play: it would be worthwhile for the benefactors collectively to increase their bequests beyond what they would be willing to make individually. See section 4.8 on intertemporal externalities in consumption and the references cited there.

last period of the present generation's life, any public debt which may be outstanding will be neutralized only if the government runs a budgetary surplus just sufficient to retire the government debt. Hence a neutral policy will make the government neither a net borrower nor a lender over the present generation's lifetime as a whole. A policy of net government borrowing over the life of the present generation would deceive people into believing that their possibilities for consuming and adding to the consumption possibilities of their heirs were greater than they really were.

We have seen that a neutral policy toward growth is Pareto-optimal from the standpoint of the present generation only if a number of stringent conditions are satisfied. No doubt the reader can produce a long list of ways in which these conditions fail to be satisfied by real-life economies. In what follows we discuss the most frequently cited and perhaps most important failures of actual market economies to satisfy these conditions. Such a discussion will, it is hoped, illuminate the meaning of these conditions and reveal their stringency. Further, the discussion may indicate how fiscal policy should depart from neutrality so as to make the allocation of resources approximate more closely to a Pareto optimum. Finally we have to examine the policy of neutrality when generations "overlap."

4.2 A False Objection: The Wage Effect of Extra Saving

Before turning to valid objections to a neutral policy, to ways in which market economies bias the rate of saving away from a Pareto-optimal level by virtue of their failure to satisfy the above conditions, we should consider the following false objection: It has been argued that in market economies in which there is no government—and, by implication, in market economies in which the government pursues a neutral policy—there is "too little saving" (less saving than is necessary for a Pareto optimum, given the distribution of income), because consumers, in deciding how much to save, do not foresee the effect on their wages of additional saving.

This argument is incorrect if the above conditions are satisfied. For under perfect markets and in the absence of externalities the rate of interest between one date and another measures the social rate of return (at the second date) to saving (at the first date). It measures the marginal "net" rate of transformation between consumption at the first date and consumption at the second date of every individual.[1] (In the absence of depreciation and embodied technical progress this social rate of return is just the *marginal productivity of capital.*)

It is true, of course, that if a finite lump of capital is added, the wage rate will increase; but as this capital is added, the rate of interest will fall: the rise of wages will be offset by the fall of quasi rents on capital already in existence. If this is taken into account, no finite increase of capital will appear attractive when an infinitesimal increase of capital does not, provided the convexity conditions implicit in a competitive equilibrium are satisfied.

If it were true that the "wage effect" of additional saving should be taken into account in saving decisions, then it would also be true that the analogous "interest effect" of increased effort should be taken into account in effort-leisure decisions. All the classical theorems, with their various assumptions, about the Pareto optimality of a competitive equilibrium would be in error.

4.3 Myopia

Perhaps the best-known objection to the market solution of the growth problem (in the absence of government or, by extension, in the presence of a neutral government policy toward growth) is the "myopia" argument advanced by Pigou. The objection relates to condition 5. Pigou wrote:[2]

Generally speaking, everybody prefers present pleasures or satisfactions of given magnitude to future pleasures or satisfactions of equal magnitude, even when the latter are perfectly certain to occur. . . . [This] implies only that our telescopic faculty is defective, and that we, therefore, see future pleasures, as it were, on a diminished scale. That this is the right explanation is proved by the fact that exactly the same diminution is experienced when, apart from our tendency to forget ungratifying incidents, we contemplate the past. Hence the existence of preference for present over equally certain future pleasures

[1] By the t-period social rate of return to saving or net marginal rate of transformation we mean the value of r which satisfies the equation $-\partial C_t/\partial C_o = (1 + r)^t$, $C_i = $ const, $i \neq 0, t$, where C_i measures the consumption in period i.

[2] A. C. Pigou, *The Economics of Welfare*, 4th ed. (London: Macmillan & Co., Ltd., 1932), pp. 24–25.

does not imply that any economic dissatisfaction would be suffered if future pleasures were substituted at full value for present ones. The non-satisfaction this year of a man's preference to consume this year rather than next year is balanced by the satisfaction of his preference next year to consume next year rather than to have consumed this year. . . . [This] implies that people distribute their resources between the present, the near future and the remote future on the basis of a wholly irrational preference.

Pigou is saying that people choose currently to consume amounts which they regret in the future. He implies that there is no feasible consumption program which the individual would not at some point in his lifetime prefer to exchange for some other feasible consumption program. If this is the correct interpretation of Pigou, then the question arises: Which preferences should be the ruling ones, those of one's youth, middle age, or old age? Pigou's own answer appears to be that none should be ruling. Instead we should take the preferences of the individual at any age (say, early age) and purge them of pure time preference. We should strive to reshape the indifference curves so as to make marginal rates of substitution along the 45° line equal to (minus) unity and presumably alter other marginal rates of substitution by an equal amount. Government policy would then be devoted to securing a growth path which is Pareto-optimal given these decontaminated preferences.

It is not clear how one would test Pigou's assertion that there is no feasible consumption program which would be preferred from the vantage point of every age in the individual's life. Even if preferences among consumption programs do differ somewhat at different ages, how important are the differences among preferred programs? Further, it seems unreasonable to expect people in their role as voters and policy makers to adopt preferences which differ from their preferences as exhibited in the marketplace.

The upshot of the Pigovian assertion, if it is correct, is that there is no Pareto optimum because there is no set of consistent preferences. But it is not obvious what the government's response to this alleged phenomenon should be.

4.4 Imperfect Forecasting of Future Prices

A fact of economic life is that comprehensive futures markets do not exist. This is not serious to the extent that people are still able to forecast correctly the future course of prices. But it is clear that people cannot forecast exactly the course of future prices. This has been argued forcefully by J. de V. Graaff:[1]

Let us abstract from such familiar difficulties as external effects in production, the dependence of production functions upon the distribution of wealth, or the presence of monopoly. Let us assume, that is to say, conditions completely favorable to the satisfactory working of the price mechanism. The amount of saving any one household undertakes (out of a given income, and at a given rate of interest) will depend upon the goods and services it expects those savings to be able to purchase in future years—upon the expected level of prices. If it holds a part of its savings in the form of bonds, expected interest rates will enter the picture; if in the form of money, the general level of prices; if in the form of durable commodities, relative prices. But the prices which will actually prevail in the future will depend upon the savings decisions of other households, now and in the future. This is so, not only on the demand side, but also because the savings decisions of all households together determine the rate of capital formation—and thus the supply of future goods and services. No one household has any way of knowing what other households intend to do. The market does not provide it with the information it requires to make a rational decision.

This is perhaps one of the more important senses in which the rate of saving (and investment) is unavoidably "political." The ordinary mechanism of the market cannot handle it. The ballot box, or something else, must be substituted for the price mechanism.

Uncertainty about the saving decisions of others is not the only cause of imperfect forecasting of future prices. Individual entrepreneurs cannot know the profitability of their investments until they know future prices (including wage rates and interest rates), and they cannot know these future prices until they know what other entrepreneurs will invest. Graaf writes:[2]

No individual entrepreneur can estimate, on the basis of [current] market data alone, the productivity of investment until the investment plans of other entrepreneurs are determined. How can one say what the productivity of investment in a particular town will be until one knows whether or not that new railway is to be laid down? We have here something analogous to external effects in production—but again something quite distinct from true external effects, since it works through the price system and has nothing to do with

[1] J. de V. Graaff, *Theoretical Welfare Economics* (London: Cambridge University Press, 1957), p. 103.
[2] *Ibid.*, p. 104.

the interrelation of production functions in a technological sense. It nevertheless leads to a similar breakdown of the ordinary price mechanism.

Thus there is another sense in which the determination of the rate of investment is unavoidably "political." If it were all undertaken by the state, or by a single entrepreneur, the difficulty would be met.

In this connection Graaff cites William Baumol, who has written:[1]

Hicks [J. R. Hicks, *Value and Capital*, 2d ed. (London: Oxford University Press, 1946), pp. 133–134] lists two categories of causes for failure to realize expectations whose potency may be decreased by central planning. First, expectations may be inconsistent, in which case it is clear that some must necessarily be disappointed; second, even if expectations are similar or even identical, the plans based on them may be inconsistent with the results anticipated. This is readily illustrated: crop prospect reports during the early part of the season may provide the farmer with some sort of guide as to the preliminary plans other farmers have made, so that he can adjust his own plans accordingly. He is, however, unable to do anything but conjecture about any changes in the plans of other farmers. Thus it becomes possible that early prospects of a relatively small crop may induce so high a prospective price that many farmers will increase their acreage to an extent leading to a glut at the end of the season. In a completely co-ordinated economy, of course, such a glut is not possible, i.e., if a glut occurs it is likely to be for other reasons.

Tjalling Koopmans has referred to this phenomenon as *secondary uncertainty*. He writes:[2]

In a rough and intuitive judgment the secondary uncertainty arising from lack of communication, that is from one decision maker having no way of finding out the concurrent decisions and plans made by others (or merely of knowing suitable aggregate measures of such decisions or plans), is quantitatively at least as important as the primary uncertainty arising from random acts of nature and unpredictable changes in consumers' preferences.

These arguments should persuade anyone of the nonoptimality of uncoordinated competitive markets. But they do not argue (nor were they intended to, we think) decisively for a collective or governmental determination of the rate of saving.

It should be clear that in the absence of centralized information about individual consumer preferences, there is no hope that the gov-

[1] William J. Baumol, *Welfare Economics and the Theory of the State* (Cambridge, Mass.: Harvard University Press, 1952), pp. 160–161.

[2] T. C. Koopmans, *Three Essays on the State of Economic Science* (New York: McGraw-Hill Book Company, 1957), pp. 162–163.

ernment, by controlling the rate of saving, can produce a Pareto-optimal growth path. Furthermore, unless policy controls radically different from the ordinary fiscal and monetary controls now in existence are used, the uncertainty as to what other households will save would merely be exchanged for uncertainty as to how much taxes the government will levy. Suppose that the government plans a certain program of capital formation and taxes so as to make aggregate consumption demand accord with this plan. It may be necessary to revise tax rates many times over in the future in order to realize the plan. If the propensities to consume of the population are not correctly predicted or if those propensities change unpredictably, taxes will have to be revised in an unpredicted way. Hence an "aggregate investment plan" engineered by conventional fiscal and monetary tools would not remove the need of each household to know what other households planned to save. Only detailed economic planning, in which the consumption of each household is planned by the government and realized by individual controls, would remove the problem.

It seems clear, therefore, that Graaff's argument is not a decisive objection to the use of a neutral policy toward growth together with competitive markets. Such an approach to the growth problem may be as good as any other in practice. It is true, however, that if we knew in what way consumers misestimated future prices we would want to deviate from a neutral policy. For example, suppose that consumers habitually underestimated future wages because they neglected sources of future productivity growth. Then they would underestimate their true "wealth" if the government conscientiously taxed in such a way as to reduce wealth by the present discounted value of planned government expenditures, i.e., if the government followed a neutral policy. To compensate for this underestimate, the government could collect taxes in amount less than the neutral level and thus make estimated disposable wealth come closer to its true value.

Another example of a failure of condition 2 to be satisfied which calls for a modification of neutral policy in a clear direction is the following: Suppose that the government plans a public investment for which no charge to users is to be made. If this public investment will contribute to the production of private consumption goods and hence will contribute positively to consumers' true wealth, then consumers should take it into account in estimating that wealth. Suppose, however, that consumers are unaware that this investment is being undertaken or are ignorant of its effect upon their wealth. Then, if a neutral policy is being pursued and if there are no other misestimations of wealth by consumers, wealth will be underestimated. Hence taxes should be reduced below the neutral level in order to raise estimated wealth to its true level. This proposition, we believe, is the grain of truth behind the idea that public investments should be debt-financed. If the effects on productivity of these investments are disregarded by consumers, tax financing of these investments may cause consumers to believe they are poorer than they really are.

We have seen that a neutral policy together with competitive markets may fail to produce a Pareto optimum by reason of imperfect knowledge of future prices and public expenditures. But no other approach to the growth problem will be Pareto-optimal either. A defensible approach is to modify neutral policy so as to compensate as well as possible for consumers' misestimates of future prices and public expenditures.

Similar remarks apply to the phenomenon of secondary uncertainty affecting individual investment decisions. A system in which investment decisions are coordinated may not be superior to an uncoordinated system. Undoubtedly there is room for more coordination of investment plans; publication of investment surveys by the government might be helpful. But one must take into account the costs of gathering and disseminating such information.

Wherever uncoordinated competitive markets are used, the question arises: How should neutral policy be modified to take into account the errors of the market arising from secondary uncertainty? While this appears at first to be an intractable problem, an important insight which may play a part in the final solution has been contributed by Tibor Scitovsky. He writes:[1]

Investment in industry A will cheapen its product; and if this is used as a factor in industry B, the latter's profits will rise. . . . The profits of

---

[1] Tibor Scitovsky, "Two Concepts of External Economies," *Journal of Political Economy*, vol. 62 (April, 1954), p. 148, quoted in Hollis B. Chenery, "The Interdependence of Investment Decisions," in Moses Abramovitz et al., *The Allocation of Economic Resources: Essays in Honor of B. F. Haley* (Stanford, Calif.: Stanford University Press, 1959), p. 84.

industry B, created by the lower price of factor A, call for investment and expansion in industry B, one result of which will be an increase in industry B's demand for industry A's product . . . equilibrium is reached only when successive doses of investment and expansion in the two industries have led to the simultaneous elimination of profits in both. It is only at this stage, where equilibrium has been established that the conclusions of equilibrium theory become applicable. . . . We can conclude, therefore, that when an investment gives rise to pecuniary external economies, its private profitability understates its social desirability.

Investments which yield "pecuniary external economies" of this sort should be subsidized by the government. By deviating from a neutral policy in this way—neutral policy will usually require that only lump-sum taxes are employed—the government can improve the allocation of resources between aggregate investment and consumption and also the allocation of resources among different investments.

4.5 Risk: Private versus Social

Both "secondary uncertainty" and "primary uncertainty," to use Koopmans' terms, lead to a malallocation of resources for another reason: atomistic producers tend to shy away from certain investments whose actuarial return justifies their being undertaken from society's point of view. In this connection, Robert Solow has written:[1]

I would like to call your attention to the fact that all the social rates of return we have talked about [those estimated by Solow for the United States and West Germany] are in the 15–20 per cent range, and perhaps even higher if we neglect housing and think mainly of business investment. If they are anywhere near right, then they suggest that rates of investment considerably higher than the current ones might be socially desirable. In the United States, many people save voluntarily to buy riskless assets paying 4 to 5 per cent annual interest. Presumably, then, large classes of people have a marginal rate of time preference no greater than 4 or 5 per cent a year. Of course, single productive investments are far from riskless, even apart from the danger of cyclical recession which is still real in the United States. But a large number of investments taken together carry a greatly reduced risk per dollar, if only they have some statistical independence, and the main requirement for that is that the business cycle not be too severe. If the whole economy can be thought of as a bank capable of paying 15–20 per cent interest, then it would

[1] Robert M. Solow, *Capital Theory and the Rate of Return* (Amsterdam: North Holland Publishing Company, 1963), p. 96.

seem to be in society's interest to find ways of making somewhat larger deposits.

And, in the same connection, James Tobin has written:[1]

Risks provide a . . . reason for the observed divergence between the rates of return satisfactory to savers and those typically required of real investment projects. Some of these are risks to the economy as well as to the owners of the business: technological hazards, uncertainties about consumer acceptance of new products, or uncertainties about the future availability and social opportunity cost of needed factors of production. Even though these are social as well as private risks, it is not clear that society should take a risk-averse position towards them and charge a risk premium against those projects entailing more uncertainties than others. Presumably society can pool such risks and realize with a very small margin of uncertainty the actuarial return on investments.

Moreover, some of the private risks are not social risks at all. Consider, for example, uncertainties about competition and market shares; if several rivals are introducing a new process or new product, the main uncertainties in the investment calculation of each are the future actions of the others. Consider, further, the high and sometimes prohibitive cost which many firms impute to external funds—apparently as insurance against loss of control to new shareowners, or, with extremely bad luck, to bond holders. If savers were offered the rates of return asked of and earned by business investments, in the form of assets that impose no more risk on the holder than is commensurate to the social risks involved, presumably they would choose to save more.

One problem to which Solow and Tobin are pointing is that expected rates of return to most savers—as measured by expected yields on bonds and stocks—are typically smaller than the expected or actuarial rates of return on real investments; investors in physical capital fail to invest up to the point where the expected rate of return is equal to the market rate of interest. This occurs because, while savers can diversify their holdings of stocks and bonds, the managers—whose self-interest is tied closely to the firms they manage rather than only to a broad number of firms—cannot diversify much, by the very nature of their management task.

Another problem is that, even if managers invested so as to equate the expected return on real investments to the rates of interest demanded on bonds and stocks by savers, the rates of interest demanded

[1] James Tobin, "Economic Growth as an Objective of Government Policy," *American Economic Review Papers and Proceedings*, vol. 54 (May, 1964), pp. 13 -14.

by savers are higher than they would be if savers could diversify without cost.

Clearly, public policy should seek to perfect the capital market, to encourage managers to serve the interests of the stockholders, and to facilitate diversification of stockholding. Perhaps government participation in the financing of firms undertaking very risky investments would be desirable.

But to the extent that an ideal solution cannot be attained, a "second-best" policy would be indicated. Such a policy might consist of subsidies to investment, particularly investments with demonstrably high variations in rates of return experienced in the past and investments in new products. These subsidies would narrow the divergence between before-subsidy expected rates of return and market rates of interest paid to savers. Market rates of interest would rise. Whether or not that rise would induce greater or less saving is, as is well known, not determinable a priori. It is true that if, for example, saving should increase, then the same increase of saving could have been brought about by a higher level of taxes on households, together with easier money. But to deviate from neutral policy by levying such higher taxes would be desirable only if it were known that this would have the same effect as investment subsidies, i.e., only if it were known that a rise of interest rates induces an increase of saving. To put the matter differently, it cannot be presumed that the objection by Solow and Tobin to competitive markets implies (given a neutral policy) that there is too little saving; that there is too much saving is an equally possible consequence of the divergence between rates of return that Solow and Tobin cite.

In conclusion, it can be agreed that the presence of risks to investment make it unlikely that competitive markets under a neutral policy will produce a Pareto optimum. But this proposition does not seem to call for the wholesale abandonment of the principle of neutrality. Rather, it calls for supplementing neutral policy, as it were, by certain investment subsidies.

4.6 Monopoly

The presence of monopoly in economies is another cause for the failure of neutral policy to be Pareto-optimal. Of particular significance for the growth problem is the fact that monopolistic firms do not invest up to the point where the rate of return on investment is equal to the rate of return available to savers. Tobin makes the following comments on this problem:[1]

A monopolistic or oligopolistic firm limits its expansion in product markets, its purchases in factor markets, and its calls on capital markets, because the firm takes into account that prices and rates in these markets will turn against it. The managers seek to maintain a market valuation of the firm in excess of the replacement cost of its assets, the difference representing the capitalized value of its monopoly power, often euphemistically called good will. Restrictions and costs of entry prevent other firms from competing this difference away. Foresighted and lucky investors receive the increases in the firm's market value in the form of capital gains. But the willingness of savers to value the assets of the firm above their cost, i.e., to supply capital at a lower rate of return than the firm earns internally, is not translated into investment either by this firm or by others. One effect is to depress rates of return in more competitive sectors of the economy. But another result is to restrict total saving and investment.

Undoubtedly the "first-best" policy would seek to eliminate monopolistic behavior (if not the monopolies or oligopolies themselves). It would take us too far afield to discuss possibly appropriate antimonopoly measures and their chances of success. An excellent summary of some ideal antimonopoly measures is given by Baumol.[2]

But if we suppose that ideal measures to eliminate monopolistic behavior are not practicable, then the problem becomes one of the second best. Investment subsidies and employment subsidies might be desirable. Taxes on personal income different from the neutral level might also be desirable. If the effect of the monopoly is to cause too much consumption and too much leisure, then an increase of taxes on households might induce less consumption and less leisure, in which case a second-best policy would involve more than neutral levels of taxes on households. But this is not necessarily the case: the monopoly, by reducing interest rates and wage rates below the marginal-value productivities of capital and labor, respectively, may produce an income effect as well as a substitution effect on saving. Consequently,

[1] *Ibid.*, p. 13.
[2] Baumol, *op. cit.*, pp. 65–72.

second-best tax policy may require a reduction of taxes on households below the neutral level.

4.7 Externalities in Production

Externalities in production—by which we mean the dependence of the production function of a firm upon inputs or outputs elsewhere in the economy—are a well-known reason for the failure of competitive markets to produce a Pareto optimum. Since we are particularly concerned with the implications of such market failures for growth policy, we shall concentrate on a kind of externality which has special relevance to investment and growth. We refer to external returns from investment.

It is clear that many kinds of investments yield benefits which are not fully captured by the individual or firm undertaking the investment. Research and development expenditures are the classic example. Since information is technically a "public good"—it can feasibly be shared by all without social cost (abstracting from any cost of transmitting the information)—there should ideally be no price charged to producers who might benefit from access to the research performed by other producers. But if firms doing research are deprived of patent protection (of the ability to charge a price to users of the research) and the government does nothing to stimulate such research, then such research will be undersupplied: it will be supplied only in the amount that is most profitable to the firms undertaking the research rather than in the amount which is most desirable for the economy as a whole. The way out of this dilemma—no price should be charged for the use of research, but failure to charge a price weakens incentives to do research—is through government finance or government subsidization of research (with little or no patent protection allowed).[1]

It is frequently argued that there is too little research done in most economies because of the difficulty experienced by the inventor of

[1] See Kenneth J. Arrow, "Economic Welfare and the Allocation of Resources for Invention," in the National Bureau of Economic Research volume, Richard R. Nelson (ed.), *The Rate and Direction of Inventive Activity* (Princeton, N.J.: Princeton University Press, 1962), and Richard R. Nelson, "The Simple Economics of Basic Scientific Research," *Journal of Political Economy*, vol. 67, no. 3 (June, 1959), pp. 297–306.

appropriating all the social benefits of the invention and because investment in new technologies is very risky. It should be clear that if we are thinking of an economy with fiscal and monetary controls, then the only safe a priori statement is that there is too little investment in technology *relative* to other kinds of investment; total investment may be too large or too small, depending upon the fiscal and monetary policies being pursued.

But even the *relative* hypothesis may not be true since governments do engage in research and they do subsidize research. In the United States, for example, government-sponsored research is considerable; and corporate research expenditures are accounted as a current cost, rather than as a capital expenditure, unlike tangible investments so that research has a tax advantage over tangible investment. So it is difficult to judge whether this hypothesis is true.

Research and development expenditure is not the only kind of investment having pronounced external returns. Outlays for the training of personnel is another obvious example: the training of its labor force by one firm may eventually benefit other firms which later employ that labor. Expenditures by individuals on their own education and training, particularly by artists and scientists, may also yield externalities, benefits which are not appropriated by the individuals acquiring the education and training. In regard to investment in human capacities, Tobin has remarked:[1] ". . . it is by no means clear that public outlays are yet sufficient to reap the external benefits involved, or even that the relevant capital markets are sufficiently developed to permit individuals to earn the private benefits."

Even investment in tangible capital may produce important external returns. We are thinking of the possibility that the production of new capital goods may involve "learning" which will increase the productivity with which resources can produce new capital goods in the future. Such a phenomenon has been modeled in a paper by Kenneth Arrow.[2] The relation of Arrow's model to external returns from investment has been nicely described by Solow:[3]

[1] Tobin, *op. cit.*, p. 14.
[2] Kenneth J. Arrow, "The Economic Implications of Learning by Doing," *Review of Economic Studies*, vol. 29 (June, 1962), pp. 155–173.
[3] Solow, *op. cit.*, pp. 66–68.

Arrow assumes . . . that each item of capital equipment represents the highest level of technology known at the time of its construction. . . . [He] postulates that technical progress arises out of experience and experience consists of gross investment. . . . In Arrow's model when there is no gross investment there is no accumulation of knowledge . . . because nothing will have been learned. . . .

As in other models, the social attractiveness of current investment is diminished by the fact that it must compete against the possibility of investment in even more productive capital goods in the future. But a wholly new element is added. A planned economy contemplating a marginal increase in current investment will take account of the fact that each such increment constitutes some "learning"; if current investment were higher, each unit of capital created during the whole future would be more productive. This is because, in the Arrow model, the technological efficiency of newly-produced capital goods depends upon the cumulative volume of gross investment in the past. This "learning" aspect adds something to the social rate of return on current investment. But in an ordinary market economy, however perfectly competitive, there is no way for a private investor to capture any part of the added productivity that his investment contributes to all future investment. It is as if all current investment involved *ipso facto* a kind of research, the results of which are automatically in the public domain, and cannot be appropriated and sold.

The result of all this is that the private rate of return on investment falls short of the social rate of return. Entirely apart from monopolistic restrictions, one must expect the rate of investment in a private-enterprise economy to be less than optimal. Most advanced economies have recognized this with respect to research and development activity itself. Public funds finance much industrial research in most such economies. The importance of Arrow's model is to suggest that there may be a case for extending similar treatment to fixed investment for similar reasons.

Several remarks on the implications of the Arrow model are in order. First, it seems to be an overstatement to say that there is no way for the private producer to capture "any part" of the added productivity that his investment contributes to all future investment. If there were only one producer in the economy, he would capture all the "external" returns. Even in multiproducer economies many of these future returns may be internal to the individual firm.

Second, it is only in a laissez-faire or *purely* private-enterprise economy that it can be concluded that the divergence between social and private rates of return makes the market-chosen rate of investment too small. Even in that case, saving may fall with a rise of the rate of interest (as would occur if the rate of interest were brought up to equality with the social rate of return on investment). Thus it must be supposed, for the conclusion to be valid, that saving is an increasing function of the rate of interest.

Third, since saving may be too great or too small as a consequence of the divergence between social and private rates of return, the best remedy is a subsidy to investment, rather than an increase of taxes (above the neutral level) on households (which would necessarily increase the rate of investment). Such a subsidy will normally raise saving and investment but could reduce saving if the resulting rise of the rate of interest discouraged saving. This subsidy is the remedy Solow appears to recommend.

Finally, as Tobin has observed, the support to which the phenomenon of "learning by doing" gives to investment subsidies is somewhat tempered by reflecting that learning may occur in the consumption-goods sector as well as the capital-goods sector of the economy. However, the learning possibilities in the consumption-goods industries are probably more limited than in the capital-goods sector, where the output is always changing form as new kinds of capital goods are designed.

By way of summary, the presence of external returns from investment calls for the introduction of subsidies to investment (in order to equate after-subsidy private rates of return to social rates of return to investment) and hence, a modification of neutral fiscal policy, rather than any radical departure from the principle of neutrality.

4.8 Externalities in Consumption

Externalities in consumption occur when the utility of an individual depends not only on his own consumption but also upon the consumptions of others. We shall concern ourselves here with an intertemporal externality in consumption which has particular significance for Pareto-optimal growth.

The argument to be set forth was first perceived by Baumol, who saw the possibility that[1] ". . . neither private interest nor altruism (except if he has grounds for assurance that others, too, will act in a manner designed to promote the future welfare of the community)

---

[1] Baumol, *op. cit.*, p. 92.

can lead [an individual] to invest for the future, and particularly the far distant future, to an extent appropriate from the point of view of the community as a whole."

The argument was later clarified by A. K. Sen, who has called the phenomenon the *isolation paradox*:[1]

Let us assume that the individual has no imperfection of knowledge about how much others will save. . . . Let us also assume that he is an individual with a constant and consistent set of preferences . . . [which do] not vary according to his position, i.e., according to whether he is acting in a political or non-political capacity. . . . The question is whether, even in these special circumstances, his saving decisions will properly reflect his views on how much should be saved by members of the present generation for the future.

Now this individual has a choice, let us say, between one unit of consumption now and three units of consumption in twenty years' time. He knows, for some reason, that in twenty years he will be dead. He cares for the future generations, but it is not enough, let us assume, to make him sacrifice a unit of his present consumption for three units for the generation living in twenty years' time. He decides, therefore, to consume the unit; but another man comes and tells him that if he saves one unit of consumption the other man will also save one unit. It would not be, by any means, irrational for the first man to change his mind now and to agree to save a unit. The gain to the future generation is much greater, and he can bring all this about by sacrificing himself only one unit of consumption. So he may, without any inconsistency, act differently in the two cases. This is a problem we may face in much larger scale in contrasting individual saving decisions with a political decision taken by the whole society. This [isolation paradox] . . . does not arise due to any inconsistency of values, but to the differences in the nature of the choice involved in the two cases. . . .

It looks as if the conflict arises because the person concerned values the gains of the future generation but does not care at all about the sacrifices of others in the present generation. This is not so. The possibility of the conflict is present whenever the person values the sacrifice (of one unit, in the above example) of present consumption of others less than the corresponding gain (three units) of the future generation, so that he would like them to save more.

The argument has been given a mathematical formulation by Stephen Marglin.[2] The simplest model analyzed by Marglin is the following:

[1] A. K. Sen, "On Optimizing the Rate of Saving," *Economic Journal*, vol. 71 (September, 1961), pp. 487–488.

[2] Stephen A. Marglin, "The Social Rate of Discount and the Optimal Rate of Investment," *Quarterly Journal of Economics*, vol. 77, no. 1 (February, 1963), pp. 95–112.

Let β denote the value which each person in the community puts on an extra unit of consumption by any of his contemporaries; that is, β indicates the increase of the individual's own consumption that would be necessary to compensate him for the loss of a unit of consumption by one of his contemporaries. An altruist would have a positive β, like 0.1.

Similarly, let α denote the value which each person in the community puts on an extra unit of consumption by any member of the next generation.

Let k be the marginal rate of transformation between present and future consumption. If capital has a positive net productivity, k will be greater than 1.

Finally, let n be the number of people both in the present community and in the future community.

Then, if everyone in the present community were to invest an additional unit (consume one unit less), so that n units were invested, the net algebraic gain from the point of view of each member of the present generation (measured in terms of his own consumption) would be

$$-1 + \alpha kn - \beta(n - 1)$$

The first term is just the loss of one unit of consumption by the individual in question. The last term measures the loss to the individual (in terms of the amount of his own consumption he would give up to avoid it) arising from the reduction by one unit of the consumption of each of the $n - 1$ other individuals in the present generation. The middle term measures the gross gain to the individual arising from the increase of future consumption by kn.

Hence each is willing to undertake the investment on the condition that everyone else also invest if and only if

$$\alpha kn \geq 1 + \beta(n - 1)$$

As Marglin observes, if n is very large, then the condition reduces to

$$\alpha k \geq \beta \quad \text{or} \quad k \geq \frac{\beta}{\alpha}$$

But it can be objected that as n becomes very large, α and β may become very small; each individual's "altruism" may become less as the number of people concerned grows larger.

In any case, there is the possibility that for some values of n there will be a net gain. And there is the possibility that for some values of n there may be a net loss. (Indeed, α may be much smaller than β for the reason that the future generation will be better off than the present generation even if no extra investment is made on their behalf so that a net loss may be the more probable result.) The significance of this, as Marglin and Sen observe, is that an atomistic market without government provides no means of bringing about the collective decrease of consumption when there is a net gain or a collective increase of consumption when there is a net loss. In such an atomistic market, actions by individuals are usually unilateral: there is no way in which the members of society can bind themselves to save more (or to save less) for the future on the condition that everyone else do the same. As Marglin observes:[1] "The coercive power of the state provides a means of enforcing the cooperation that we all desire, of ensuring that each of us bears his share of the investment burden instead of attempting to shift it onto the shoulders of others."

But precisely what the government should do to rectify the market solution is by no means clear. It must be supposed that the government does not have centralized information on peoples' utility functions at its disposal. How can the government ascertain that there would be a net gain or net loss from investing "for the future" at a greater rate? Possibly the community can communicate its wishes by pronouncements or by the ballot box. But even then there arises the question of what government policies would be best suited to satisfy the collective wish for a redistribution of consumption from the present to the next generation.

One policy which should be considered is a rise of general tax rates so as to discourage present consumption. But the objective is not to trade present for future consumption of the present generation but, rather, to trade lifetime consumption of the present generation for consumption of future generations. Undoubtedly there is some time path of tax rates on household income which will produce the desired path, but what is it?

[1] *Ibid.*, p. 104.

Perhaps the most natural policy to adopt in answer to a popular desire for intergeneration redistribution is the subsidization (or taxation) of bequests, it being left for the future government to decide upon the distribution of income of the future generation. Such a policy could supplement an otherwise neutral tax policy.

But while the vestiges of a neutral policy might thereby be preserved, the essential point is that if the Baumol-Sen-Marglin externalities are appreciable, then the government can no longer count on perfect markets in combination with a neutral policy toward growth to bring about a Pareto optimum. It must listen to the political voice of the community, not merely rely on the community's market actions, if a Pareto-optimal growth path is to be achieved. It is important to know, therefore, whether these intertemporal externalities are large enough to be worth considering.

4.9 Neutrality Examined When Generations Overlap

Up to this point, we have supposed that there is no overlapping of generations: each generation arrived on the scene only after the previous generation died. An important property of models of this kind is that the present generation cannot consume over its life more than the consumption goods it produces over its life because it cannot acquire goods produced by the next generation. But it may be possible for the present generation to consume some of the goods produced by the next generation when generations overlap, as we shall show presently. This possibility will, under certain circumstances, enable the present generation to do "better" than it can do by pursuit of a neutral policy. Under other circumstances, a neutral policy may still be Pareto-optimal from the standpoint of the present generation.

Suppose that the present generation—those living now—survive into the period in which new people enter the labor force. We shall refer to these new entrants as the *next generation*.

Clearly the government in power during the period in which the two generations coexist can redistribute income between the two generations, the old and the new. That government cannot be neutral toward the intergeneration distribution of after-tax income in the sense of leaving that distribution up to the market; it could be "neutral" only in the sense of following an ethical criterion such as "equal treatment."

The present generation and the government in power before the new generation enters the economy will have to take into account the policies of the next government if the present generation is to achieve a Pareto-optimal path of consumption and bequests. In particular, the present government will modify its notion of neutrality toward growth. A neutral policy by the present government will no longer seek to impoverish the present generation by the total amount of the government expenditures which are to be made during the lifetime of the present generation; for the costs of the public goods provided when the old and new generations coexist may be absorbed partly by the new generation. Rather, leaving any initial debt aside for simplicity, a neutral policy on the part of the present government will tax so as to reduce expected wealth by the amount of the (discounted) cost of all government expenditures made before the new generation arrives *plus* the discounted net taxes which are expected (by the government) to be levied on the old generation by the next government. (If the taxpayers of the present generation have the same expectations about taxes to be levied by the next government as does the present government, then the latter need not levy any taxes to reduce wealth on this account since those future taxes are already being considered by the taxpayers.[1])

But in this case of overlapping generations, it is possible, indeed there is some presumption, that a neutral policy will not be Pareto-optimal from the standpoint of the present generation, quite aside from the presence of the market imperfections and externalities discussed above. To illustrate this possibility, let us suppose that no one of the present generation "cares" for any member of the next generation, or more precisely, that bequests have no utility per se and that utility is independent of the behavior of every member of the next generation. Then the present government may be able to improve the consumption possibilities, and hence increase the utility, of the

---

[1] If the new generation is defined in such a way that it enters the labor force next year, then this definition of neutral taxation calls for net taxes equal to this year's government expenditures plus the initial government debt if taxes expected next year are exogenous.

present generation by issuing interest-bearing debt before the new generation enters the labor force. (It could issue this debt, for example, by making debt-financed transfer payments to the population.) For the present generation can sell this debt to members of the next generation when the latter have entered the labor force and begun to earn income; the present generation can exchange this debt in return for goods and services produced by the next generation. Thus the present generation may be able to increase its consumption possibilities at the expense of the next generation. In effect it is making a "negative bequest." On the supposition that the present generation does not feel altruistic toward members of the next generation, this negative bequest will clearly increase the utility of the present generation.

The point that one generation can increase its consumption at the expense of the next by means of exchanging government debt for goods produced by the next generation appears to have been made first by William Bowen, Richard Davis, and David Kopf.[1] The point that this intergeneration transfer can make possible a negative bequest was made by William Vickrey.[2]

It should not be concluded from the above argument that the issue of debt is necessarily superior to a neutral policy from the point of view of the present generation. We were careful to say that the present generation "may" be able to increase its consumption possibilities at the expense of the next generation. One reservation that should be made is that the government in power when the new generation enters the labor force may offset or even reverse the transfer of goods between the two generations. That government might be able to levy additional taxes on the old generation and reduce taxes levied on the new generation. Even if it were unconstitutional to tax different generations at different rates, the government could discriminate against the old generation from the expenditure side: it could reduce transfer payments to the old generation such as retirement benefits. The government

---

[1] W. G. Bowen, R. G. Davis, and D. H. Kopf, "The Public Debt: A Burden on Future Generations?" *American Economic Review*, vol. 50, no. 4 (September, 1960), pp. 701–706.

[2] William Vickrey, "The Burden of the Public Debt: Comment," *American Economic Review*, vol. 51, no. 1 (March, 1961), pp. 132–137.

could thwart the consumption plans of the old by raising general tax rates for the remaining life of the old generation. Conceivably the government could even repudiate the public debt on the ground that it constituted a theft of property rightfully belonging to the new generation. Thus the next government could prevent the old generation from gaining at the expense of the new.

Another reservation to the proposition that the issue of debt will necessarily increase the utility of the present generation should be made when the present generation cares about the welfare of members of the next generation. Suppose that every member of the old generation has heirs, people of the next generation with whose welfare he is sufficiently concerned that he wishes to leave them bequests. Then the issue of the public debt may deceive the old generation into believing it can consume more without leaving less real capital to its heirs. If the issue of the debt causes the heirs of the next generation to inherit less real capital than they would have inherited had the old generation had full information about the consumption possibilities of its heirs, then the utility of the present generation must be judged to have declined. (Note, however, that the old generation may die believing that it has done as well by its heirs as it wished to do. This raises the somewhat philosophical question of whether we can say that the utility of the old generation has declined when it is fooled into thinking it has increased. It seems to us that we can.)

It has been argued by some writers that, in fact, the issue of debt will not cause the old generation to increase its consumption at the expense of the next. It is argued that the old generation will increase its aggregate bequest by the amount of the government bonds issued, rather than increase its consumption. James Elliott appears to find such behavior plausible. He writes:[1]

The older members of any economy which incorporates the principles of private property and the right of transfer are always free to sell their creditor claims. The sale may be made to Generation I [the old generation] or Generation II [the new generation]. If, during the lifetime of Generation I, there had been no deficit finance, they would still be free to liquidate *other* forms of creditor claims—life insurance, industrial bonds, common stock, etc.

[1] J. R. Elliott, "The Burden of the Public Debt: Comment," *American Economic Review,* vol. 51, no. 1 (March, 1961), p. 139.

Carl Shoup apparently agreed when he wrote:[1]

When one thinks of the mass of capital instruments that Generation I owns, and which it can sell to Generation II in exchange for consumption goods that Generation II was going to consume, does the existence of an extra block of financial assets . . . really make an appreciable difference?

Perhaps this argument can be expressed as follows: If the members of the old generation had wished to consume more and thus force their heirs to consume less, they could have done so without a government debt; they could simply have reduced their bequests by selling an extra amount of financial assets to the next generation. Therefore, the presence of additional financial assets (government bonds) will not induce them to consume more since they already had that opportunity and they revealed a preference not to consume more.

The unorthodoxy of this argument can be appreciated by reflecting that if it were true, then the marginal propensity to consume disposable income created by a tax reduction or transfer payment would be zero; the marginal propensity to bequeath such an increase of disposable income would be unitary.

The trouble with the argument is that it fails to recognize that taxes, transfers, and public debt can, to use Ricardo's words, blind us to our real situation. The members of the present generation may not realize that their respective heirs are made worse off by a tax reduction unless they compensate their heirs by adding sufficiently to their bequest. In the aggregate, the old generation must bequeath the whole of any tax reduction if the new generation is not to end up consuming less. There seems to be no general presumption that bequests would be so increased.

The possibility that the entire debt issued to the old generation would be entirely bequeathed to the next generation would seem to require that the next government levy taxes on the heirs of the old generation sufficient to neutralize the public debt. In this way the next government could signal the old generation that their heirs must be bequeathed the whole of the debt if the heirs are not to be worse off.

But such action by the next government may not be sufficient. First, if consumption by the old generation is not to increase at the time the debt was created, the old generation must anticipate that additional

[1] C. S. Shoup, "Debt Financing and Future Generations," *Economic Journal*, vol. 72 (December, 1962), p. 892.

taxes are going to be levied on their heirs on account of the debt. The realization by the old generation that their heirs are going to bear heavier taxes may come too late in that the old generation may, by that time, already have consumed some of their capital.

Second, it may be the size of the bequest itself of which utility is a function, rather than the expected welfare of the heirs. If so, the bequest which each member of the old generation makes to his heirs may not increase sufficiently to compensate the heirs for the higher taxes imposed on them.

Third, some of the beneficiaries of the debt-creating tax reductions or transfer payments may not wish to bequeath in any case. The rise of their consumption will necessarily be at the expense of the next generation unless their contemporaries not only refrain from consuming more but actually consume less so that their heirs will not suffer any loss of consumption.

Our conclusion is not that the present government can or cannot, by debt financing, effect a transfer of goods from the new to the old generation, but rather that the final outcome of such debt financing depends upon the response of the next government to such action (and to the present generation's expectations of that response). Even those of the present generation who have no concern for the welfare of others may not gain from debt-financed transfer payments to them or reduction of their taxes because the next government may penalize them (and their contemporaries) by higher taxes or reduced transfer payments in the future. Similarly, even those of the next generation who are not heirs may not lose, because the next government may redistribute to them some income of the old generation.

Perhaps it is not farfetched to view the present government as being in a bargaining situation with the next government in which the former government seeks the best outcome for the present generation. The present generation may do best in this game if they can show that their government has pursued a neutral policy toward growth rather than attempting to "steal" the produce of the next generation.

4.10 The Practicality of a Neutral Policy

We have seen that externalities and market imperfections may make a neutral policy toward growth nonoptimal. We have seen also that a neutral policy may also be nonoptimal from the standpoint of the present generation when generations overlap. The conditions under which a neutral policy will be Pareto-optimal from the standpoint of the present generation are stringent. Nevertheless there may remain considerable academic interest and possibly some practical interest in the question of whether a neutral policy or an approximately neutral policy could be carried out by the government.

One possible obstacle to neutrality is the unavailability of lump-sum taxes. On this point Tobin writes:[1]

The quest for neutrality is probably a search for a will-of-the-wisp. For it is not only the overall budgetary position of government, but also the specifics of taxation . . . which affect intertemporal choices. . . . It will suffice to remind you that our methods of taxation necessarily favor one kind of current consumption, leisure, both as against other current consumption and as against future consumption of products and leisure.

The problem can be stated as follows: Consider the neutral level of lump-sum taxes (corresponding to some path of planned government expenditures). Associated with the resulting equilibrium is a certain amount of investment and a certain level of leisure. But suppose now that the government has only an income tax at its disposal and that if income taxes are equated to the neutral level of lump-sum taxes then, because of substitution effects, the level of private saving (hence investment) and the level of effort are smaller than their respective neutral levels. To bring the level of investment up to the neutral level, the government need only raise income tax rates; but this action may reduce further the level of effort. It is for this reason that we concluded in Chapter 2 that neutrality was not generally possible with an income tax. But we should emphasize the word "generally": there may be exceptions. An increase of the income tax rate will increase rather than decrease effort if the income effect dominates the substitution effect. Hence it is possible, as an exception, that by setting income taxes above the neutral lump-sum level, the government can raise both total investment and effort up to their neutral levels. But the major point to be made is that *approximate* neutrality is not necessarily precluded by the absence of lump-sum taxes. By taxing above the neutral lump-sum

[1] Tobin, *op. cit.*, p. 12.

level the government may be able to bring investment and effort tolerably close to their neutral levels. The difficulty lies in the government's not knowing by how much income taxes should be set above the neutral lump-sum level.

Another obstacle to fiscal neutrality arises if the central bank's controls over aggregate demand take effect only with a lag. It is widely agreed that monetary actions take at least several months before they become effective. If that is so, then it may be necessary for the fiscal authorities to reduce taxes below the neutral level in order to counteract or forestall a fall of aggregate demand and employment. This assumes, of course, that a tax reduction will have effect upon aggregate demand quicker than will monetary actions. Similarly, if inflationary pressures occur or threaten, it may be necessary to raise taxes above the neutral level because monetary measures would not be effective soon enough.

A somewhat similar problem confronts those who would balance the budget and maintain full employment at the same time. Deficits or surpluses may be required at least temporarily.

At best, therefore, the monetary authorities can seek only to manipulate their controls so as to cause the level of taxes which is expected to be necessary in the future to secure full employment at that time to be equal to the neutral level. Thus, if the lag is x months, the central bank should act now to make equal to zero the deflationary gap which would be expected in x months' time to occur if taxes were then at the neutral level. (Note, incidentally, that bygones should be bygones: the necessity to tax below the neutral level currently does not imply that the government should aim to tax above the neutral level in the future; it should aim for neutrality in the future, which implies, of course, that any debt issued in the interim will be neutralized.) It is clear, therefore, that to the extent forecasting is imperfect, exact neutrality will not be possible.

Perhaps the primary obstacle to neutrality is the difficulty in finding the neutral level of taxes, even if lump-sum taxes should be available. Locating the neutral level requires knowledge of what households will expect to pay in taxes in the future. If taxes are based on income, this requires knowledge of what taxpayers expect their future incomes to be. In the absence of reliable consumer-survey information, a government seeking neutrality would have to be content to estimate the impact upon expected wealth of various income tax rates (or rate schedules). Thus only an approximation to neutrality can be hoped for.

As a consequence of the above, there would remain considerable debate over the level of taxes even in an economy committed to neutrality toward growth. But the debate will be over the question of whether or not present taxes on households reflect accurately the discounted value of present and future government expenditures, rather than over the question of whether or not present tax rates produce the desired rate of growth as judged from political or other expressions by the public.

4.11 A Question of Ethics

Throughout this study we have been weighing growth policies on the criterion of whether they are (Pareto-) optimal from the standpoint of the present generation. But this is not the only criterion which has been advanced. Another criterion, and perhaps the prevailing one in the minds of most contemporary economists, is *maximum social welfare*, where social welfare is a function of the welfare of each generation in a way which is governed by some ethic which may or may not be shared by the present population.

The latter view was perhaps first articulated by Pigou, who wrote:[1]

Since human life is limited, such fruits of work or saving as accrue after a considerable interval are not enjoyed by the person to whose efforts they are due. . . . It follows that, even though our desires for equal satisfactions *of our own* occurring at different times were equal, our desire for future satisfaction would often be less intense than for present satisfaction, because it is very likely that the future satisfaction will not be our own. . . . The practical way in which these discrepancies between desire and satisfaction work themselves out to the injury of economic welfare is by checking the creation of new capital and encouraging people to use up existing capital to such a degree that large future advantages are sacrificed for smaller present ones.

In essence Pigou is saying that each generation bequeaths to the next less than the socially optimal amount of capital because each generation assigns less weight to the utilities of future people than *ought* to be assigned—than are assigned by Pigou's social welfare function.

[1] A. C. Pigou, *The Economics of Welfare*, 4th ed. (London: Macmillan & Co., Ltd., 1932), p. 26.

It seems to be implicit in what Pigou says that the utility or the consumption level of the representative man in each generation receives equal weight in the social welfare function. This is also argued by Frank Ramsey in the paper presenting his "solution" to the problem of socially optimal growth. He asserts that to "discount" the utilities of future people relative to the utilities of present people (independently of the relative magnitudes of those utilities) would be "ethically indefensible"; he held that "pure" time discounting "arises merely from the weakness of imagination."[1]

According to the Pigovian position, then, the government ought to serve the interests of succeeding generations as well as the interests of the present generation. This seems innocuous enough, but in fact it is controversial. It is an authoritarian solution to the problem of growth. The social welfare function is to be constructed according to ethical tenets which may not be shared by a single member of the community. It is difficult to see how maximization of a social welfare function which does not reflect *only* the interests (be they altruistic or selfish) of the present generation can be carried out by a government which is "democratic." Marglin argues the point well:[2]

I, for one, do not accept the Pigovian formulation of social welfare. If I am going to play the neoclassical, or rather neo-Benthamite, game, in which individuals are assumed to have well-defined preferences that are identical to their utilities, I want to play the rest of the bourgeois-democratic game of philosophical liberalism as well: in particular I want the government's social welfare function to reflect only the preferences of present individuals. Whatever else democratic theory may or may not imply, I consider it axiomatic

---

[1] F. P. Ramsey, "A Mathematical Theory of Saving," *Economic Journal,* vol. 38 (December, 1928), p. 543.

[2] Marglin, *op. cit.*, p. 97.

Marglin would favor the government's educating the citizenry to the "rightful claims" of future generations, with the proviso that "if after being made aware of future needs, present individuals remain indifferent to the claims of future individuals, then, it seems to me, a democratic view of the state does not countenance governmental intervention on behalf of future generations" (*ibid.*, p. 98). Even this may be outside democratic bounds however; if the people do not wish to be exposed to propaganda or courses in ethics, then the government cannot provide them and at the same time cater only to the preferences of the present generation. Such education could be justified, however, on the paternalistic ground that the present generation's true interests and preferences were not identical.

that a democratic government reflects only the preferences of the individuals who are presently members of the body politic.

Needless to say, the identification of the Pigou-Ramsey solution as "authoritarian" does not ineluctably condemn that solution. Democracy is presumably not the highest goal. If one shares the conviction of Pigou and Ramsey, he might reasonably wish to trade some democracy in return for the realization of his other ethical principles. For ourselves, we shall say only that Pareto optimality from the standpoint of the present generation is a criterion that is certainly not beneath consideration. It should not, it seems to us, be rejected out of hand.

4.12 Conclusions

If democratic governments must interest themselves only in the preferences of the present generation, then the fundamental problem of growth for such governments is to find those fiscal and monetary policies which are Pareto-optimal from the standpoint of the present generation. We have been examining one candidate for such a status, namely, a fiscal-monetary policy of neutrality toward growth. The fisc and central bank were said to be neutral if they produced the same allocation of resources over time as would be produced if there were no fisc and no central bank but, instead, only an agency to conscript resources for government use, an agency to redistribute wealth, and a private monopoly bank which "priced" its services (including liquidity) in a Pareto-optimal way.

We found that if generations did not overlap, a neutral policy would be Pareto-optimal in the absence of externalities and market imperfections. In those circumstances, a nonneutral policy would cause expected disposable wealth to differ from the present discounted value of the preferred consumption plan, with the consequence that the preferred plan would not be chosen.

But market imperfections and externalities prevail in all actual economies. There is imperfect knowledge of future prices and future government expenditures. Imperfections of capital markets lead to discrimination against investments which carry high private risks. Monopolies clearly create a divergence between private and social rates of return to investment. So do the external effects of certain kinds of investment, especially investment in new technology. Finally, there may be important externalities in consumption of the intertemporal kind analyzed by Sen and Marglin.

These imperfections and externalities raise the question of how government policy, particularly fiscal policy, can be employed to reduce or eliminate the resulting malallocations of resources. One possibility is the wholesale abandonment of fiscal-monetary neutrality in favor of comprehensive economic planning for growth. We suggested instead that the principle of neutrality be modified: we proposed the introduction of various subsidies of certain investments and possibly of bequests. But exact Pareto optimality in the face of these imperfections and externalities is clearly beyond reach.

Perhaps the most fundamental defect of neutrality arises when generations overlap. In that situation the present generation, by suitable fiscal policy, may be able to consume more than the wealth they inherit and produce over their own lifetime (net of the wealth diverted for government use). The government in power before the arrival of the next generation, by issuing debt to the present generation, would enable the present generation to sell that debt to the next generation in return for goods and services produced by the next generation. There is no certainty, however, that this device will increase the utility of the present generation.

First, if the issue of the debt, by inducing people of the present generation to consume more, causes them to bequeath less real capital to the next generation than they would have done had they had full information about the consumption possibilities of their heirs, then their utility must be judged to have declined on that account. On the other hand, if people of the present generation wish to make a "negative bequest" of real capital to some or all people of the next generation and if the issue of debt enables them to increase their consumption at the expense of those people, then the utility of the present generation will increase on that account. (But if there are externalities of the type such that each individual does not wish to see his contemporaries gain at the expense of the next generation, then this negative bequest to nonheirs may not be utility-increasing after all, even though each individual might like to make a negative bequest if he could do it alone.)

However, the government in power when the next generation arrives has considerable power over the distribution of income between old and young. It may be able to nullify any gain to the old generation and even to punish the old generation for its efforts to take from the new. First, by taxing the heirs in the new generation the government may be able to induce the old generation to bequeath the whole of the debt issued to it. But some members of the old generation may not respond by bequeathing more; they may wish to bequeath nothing in any case, or it may be the size of the bequest per se that has utility, rather than the expected disposable wealth of the heirs. Second, the government taking power when the new generation appears may be able to reverse the intergeneration redistribution of income by taxing or spending in a way which discriminates against the old generation. It might even repudiate the debt on the ground that it had been issued in order to steal from the new generation rather than as a "bill" for services rendered, such as winning a war or contributing to the technology. Evidently, if the present generation contemplates consuming part of the produce of the next generation, it must consider itself in a bargaining situation in which its objective is to win some concession from the government which comes into power when the new generation arrives. The old generation may do best in this game if it can argue that its government has pursued a neutral policy, that it has "carried its own weight" in the sense of taxing so as to reduce expected disposable wealth (and hence its lifetime consumption) by the value of its lifetime government expenditures and initial public debt, rather than attempting to consume at the expense of those members of the new generation who were not compensated by additional bequests.

It seems clear that there is no hope for the optimality of so simple a policy as neutrality in a complex world. Much can be said for it in a world in which generations do not overlap, the economy is highly competitive, people are astute and unreasonably lucky at forecasting, and externalities are of negligible importance. But where generations overlap, as they do, and where externalities, especially externalities in consumption, are rampant, as they may be, there seems to be little merit in a policy of neutrality. Whatever the reader's evaluation may be, he will conclude, no doubt, that the subject of appropriate fiscal and monetary policies for growth remains a fertile one for intellectual inquiry.

Bibliography

Arrow, Kenneth J.: "The Economic Implications of Learning by Doing," *Review of Economic Studies*, vol. 29 (June, 1962), pp. 155–173.

———: "Economic Welfare and the Allocation of Resources for Invention," in Richard R. Nelson (ed.), *The Rate and Direction of Inventive Activity* (Princeton, N.J.: Princeton University Press and National Bureau of Economic Research, 1962).

Atkinson, F. J.: "Saving and Investment in a Socialist State," *Review of Economic Studies*, vol. 15, no. 2 (1947–1948), pp. 78–83.

Bailey, Martin J.: *National Income and the Price Level* (New York: McGraw-Hill Book Company, 1962).

———: "The Welfare Cost of Inflationary Finance," *Journal of Political Economy*, vol. 64 (April, 1956), pp. 93–110.

Baumol, William J.: *Welfare Economics and the Theory of the State* (Cambridge, Mass.: Harvard University Press, 1952).

Becker, Gary S.: "Underinvestment in College Education?" *American Economic Review*, vol. 50 (May, 1960), pp. 346–354.

Bowen, William G., Richard G. Davis, and David H. Kopf: "The Public Debt: A Burden on Future Generations?" *American Economic Review*, vol. 50 (September, 1960), pp. 701–706.

Elliott, James R.: "The Burden of the Public Debt: Comment," *American Economic Review*, vol. 51 (March, 1961), pp. 139–140.

Graaff, Jan de V.: *Theoretical Welfare Economics* (London: Cambridge University Press, 1957).

Hicks, John R.: *Value and Capital*, 2d ed. (London: Oxford University Press, 1946).

Keynes, John Maynard: *The General Theory of Employment, Interest, and Money* (London: Macmillan & Co., Ltd., 1936).

Koopmans, Tjalling C.: *Three Essays on the State of Economic Science* (New York: McGraw-Hill Book Company, 1957).

Lerner, Abba P.: *The Economics of Control* (New York: The Macmillan Company, 1945).

Marglin, Stephen A.: "The Social Rate of Discount and the Optimal Rate of Investment," *Quarterly Journal of Economics*, vol. 77 (February, 1963), pp. 95–112.

Meade, James E.: "Is the National Debt a Burden?" *Oxford Economic Papers*, vol. 10 (June, 1958).

Metzler, Lloyd A.: "Wealth, Saving and the Rate of Interest," *Journal of Political Economy*, vol. 59 (April, 1951), pp. 93–116.

Modigliani, Franco: "Long-run Implications of Alternative Fiscal Policies and the Burden of the National Debt," *Economic Journal*, vol. 71 (December, 1961), pp. 730–755.

Nelson, Richard R.: "The Simple Economics of Basic Scientific Research," *Journal of Political Economy*, vol. 67 (June, 1959), pp. 297–306.

Phelps, Edmund S.: "Anticipated Inflation and Economic Welfare," *Journal of Political Economy*, vol. 73 (February, 1965), pp. 1–13.

———: "The New View of Investment: A Neoclassical Analysis," *Quarterly Journal of Economics*, vol. 76 (November, 1962), pp. 548–567.

———: "Substitution, Fixed Proportions, Growth and Distribution," *International Economic Review*, vol. 4 (September, 1963), pp. 265–288.

Pigou, Alfred C.: *The Economics of Welfare*, 4th ed. (London: Macmillan & Co., Ltd., 1932).

Ramsey, Frank P.: "A Mathematical Theory of Saving," *Economic Journal*, vol. 38 (December, 1928), pp. 542–559.

Ricardo, David: *Principles of Political Economy* (New York: E. P. Dutton & Co., Inc., Everyman's Library, 1911).

Samuelson, Paul A.: *Economics: An Introductory Analysis*, 5th ed. (New York: McGraw-Hill Book Company, 1961).

————: "The New Look in Tax and Fiscal Policy," in *Federal Tax Policy for Economic Growth and Stability*, Subcommittee on Tax Policy, Joint Committee on the Economic Report, 84th Cong. (1955), pp. 229–234.

Scitovsky, Tibor: "Two Concepts of External Economies," *Journal of Political Economy*, vol. 62 (April, 1954).

Sen, A. K.: "On Optimising the Rate of Saving," *Economic Journal*, vol. 71 (September, 1961), pp. 479–497.

Shoup, Carl S.: "Debt Financing and Future Generations," *Economic Journal*, vol. 72 (December, 1962), pp. 887–898.

Solow, Robert M.: *Capital Theory and the Rate of Return* (Amsterdam: North Holland Publishing Company, 1963).

————: "A Contribution to the Theory of Economic Growth," *Quarterly Journal of Economics*, vol. 70 (February, 1956), pp. 65–94.

————: "Investment and Technical Progress," in K. J. Arrow, S. Karlin, and P. Suppes (eds.), *Mathematical Methods in the Social Sciences 1959* (Stanford, Calif.: Stanford University Press, 1960).

————: "Technical Progress, Capital Formation, and Economic Growth," *American Economic Review, Papers and Proceedings*, vol. 52 (May, 1962), pp. 76–86.

Swan, Trevor W.: "Economic Growth and Capital Accumulation," *Economic Record*, vol. 20 (November, 1956), pp. 334–361.

Tobin, James: "A Dynamic Aggregative Model," *Journal of Political Economy*, vol. 62 (April, 1955), pp. 103–115.

————: "Economic Growth as an Objective of Government Policy," *American Economic Review, Papers and Proceedings*, vol. 54 (May, 1964), pp. 1–20.

Vickrey, William F.: "The Burden of the Public Debt: Comment," *American Economic Review*, vol. 51 (March, 1961), pp. 132–137.

Index